AFRICA'S DIAMONDS

Yvonne Davy

May you be jewels in
His crown —
Love —
Yvonne Davy —

Pacific Press Publishing Association
Mountain View, California
Oshawa, Ontario

Designed by Ichiro Nakashima
Cover photo by Joan Walter

Copyright 1983 by
Pacific Press Publishing Association
Printed In United States of America
All rights reserved

Library of Congress Cataloging in Publication Data

Davy, Yvonne.
  Africa's Diamonds.

1. Campbell, James Rossier. 2. Campbell, Myrtle, 1889-
1982. 3. Missionaries—United States—Biography. 4. Missionaries—South Africa—Biography. 5. Seventh-day Ad-
ventists—Biography. I. Title.
BV3625.S67C353   1982   266'.676'0922   [B]82-18942
ISBN 0-8163-0512-9

FOREWORD

This little book is lovingly dedicated to the memory of Rossier and Myrtle Campbell, not only for all they did for Africa, but for all they've meant to the Davy family as well.

Much of the material I used comes from "Granny Campbell's" manuscript: "Autobiographical Sketches Highlighting the Making of a Missionary and Forty Years of Mission Service in South and Central Africa."

I also owe a debt of special thanks to Dr. H. E. Douglass, Pacific Press book editor in chief, for his kind encouragement with this task.

Contents

The Making of a Missionary

Myrtle Henry felt very new and shy as she walked across from the girls' dormitory to the administration building. Could she be the only new girl on the campus? Just then she heard hurried footsteps behind her, and turned her head to see a girl following her.

The girl called, "Wait for me. Are you going to register now?"

Myrtle nodded. "Do you know what we're supposed to do? Where we're supposed to go?" she asked.

"No. I thought you did; that's why I tried to catch up to you."

"Well, we're both ignorant, so let's go together. My name's Myrtle Henry. What's yours?"

"I'm Betty Smith. What are you planning to take?"

"I want to be a teacher," Myrtle replied. "And you?"

"It's secretarial for me. It's a shorter course. Say, did you notice that the school offers an elective called survey of missions? I feel like signing up for it."

"So do I," Myrtle Henry said to her new friend. "Ever since I was a tiny tot in Sabbath School I've been thrilled by mission stories. Who knows, I might be able to go as a teacher to Africa someday." Myrtle paused, and then with a laugh added, "First I guess we'd better get signed up. There's a man coming down the steps of that building." She pointed. "Let's ask him if he knows where we are supposed to go to register."

The man, the girls soon learned, was on the faculty. He courteously showed them to which building they should go. Once directed it didn't take them long to get into the registration line and complete their registration.

"I got the elective class survey of missions," Myrtle confided to her new friend when they met outside the administration building. "I have a really full program, that's for sure. How did you make out?"

"Fine. I've got a full program too. Unfortunately I couldn't take survey of missions. Come on, let's spend the day exploring the campus and finding some other new students around here."

The first day of classes, Myrtle found the survey of missions the smallest of her classes. There were only ten students—nine girls and one boy. Myrtle noticed that eight of the girls tried in every way to get the attention of the young man. Myrtle herself felt drawn to the young fellow whose name was James Rossier Campbell. Everyone called him Rossier. "An intelligent, handsome, quick-witted, and friendly person," Myrtle thought, but being a very proper lass she kept her feelings to herself. However, with all the attention given him by the other girls, she couldn't help feeling flattered when he seemed always to sit beside her or just behind her.

One day Rossier walked out of class beside her and asked, "What made you join the mission survey class, Miss Henry?"

"Years ago I read a thrilling book on missions, and right then I made up my mind that I was going into mission service," Myrtle responded.

"Any preference as to where you'd like to work?" Rossier asked.

"To tell the truth, my eye has been on Africa, the land of David Livingstone." Myrtle warmed to her subject and went on to tell Rossier about her dream of a lifework.

When she paused for a moment, Rossier smiled and said, "When you talk about the country of your preference, you have a delightful sparkle to your eyes."

"Don't flatter me, Mr. Campbell," she retorted.

"No flattery. It's true. And my name's Rossier. Please don't be so formal and call me mister. Has anyone told you your hairstyle is most becoming?"

"Ah, now that I won't call flattery; it's the nicest compliment you could have paid me, Mr. Rossier. Thank you. You see, I was very ill several months ago and was on the verge of losing all my hair as a result. My uncle is a barber, and he took it upon himself to practically *shave* my head. I was horrified when I saw the result. You've no idea how dreadful I looked with an 'egghead.' I think I'd have *died* with embarrassment if I'd had to come to school looking like that. Fortunately my hair grows very rapidly. I'm thankful you think it looks decent now!"

"It's beautiful—such lustrous, dark ringlets." He reached over and touched a curl lightly. "Would you mind if I called you Myrtle?"

What could she say to such a request from such a charming young man as Rossier? And so their friendship began. They spent many hours during the school year discussing their ambitions. After a while both of them wrote their parents about their friendship and of their hopes to enter mission service in Africa, for strangely enough, Africa was Rossier's first love as well as Myrtle's.

9

Myrtle worked in the kitchen at the school preparing the evening meal. Many of the students skipped this meal, but there was one young man who never missed a supper. Of course it was Rossier Campbell. He took full advantage of the chance to visit with Myrtle after he'd eaten.

One evening he asked her to sell him a pound of dates to take to his room.

"Since you've asked so nicely I most certainly will," she replied with a smile and a mock curtsy. She measured out the fruit, and then, because it was for Rossier, she dipped into the container and took the fattest, juiciest date and added it to his packet for good measure.

As she tidied up after the students had all left, the supervisor stepped up to her. "I know you didn't mean to do wrong, but you took what belongs to the kitchen and gave it to your boyfriend," she said.

Myrtle was stunned. "How? When?" she stuttered.

"When you added that extra date to Rossier's package. Think it over, my dear. You can't afford to be lax even in little things."

Impulsively the girl threw her arm around the woman. "I'm sorry," she whispered. "I just never thought of that as—as stealing!"

"I know you didn't, but I love you too well to let something like that slip by."

The next time Rossier asked to buy dates, she measured them out carefully, then took out the biggest one and put it back in the can.

"Hey, what's up? Are you trying to tell me something?" he asked somewhat mystified.

"I later realized I did wrong when I gave you the extra date the last time you bought dates, so now I'm correcting my mistake. I've felt terrible ever since. Now

I'm much happier. Will you forgive me?" she asked with a tremulous smile.

"You could take half the packet if that would make you happy," he replied, and by the look that accompanied his words the girl knew he meant it.

One day as Myrtle sat studying in the chapel, the principal, Professor Lucas, came in and looked around. Myrtle saw him look her way and then make his way over to her.

"Myrtle, I understand you and Rossier Campbell are comtemplating marriage and then service in Africa," he said after a few words of greeting.

"Yes, sir," she answered, blushing furiously.

He seemed not to notice her embarrassment. "What if the General Conference gives you a call to China while they send Rossier to India?"

Her heart skipped a beat. Did the man know something she did not? She hesitated a moment as she weighed her answer. Finally with the hint of a sigh she answered, "I guess I'd go to China if that was where God wanted me. You see, Professor, my first allegiance is to my Saviour."

He smiled kindly. "You've truly dedicated yourself to Him, haven't you!" He got up and left without another word.

Myrtle couldn't study with her mind in such a turmoil. Didn't God want her to marry Rossier? She went to her room and threw herself on her bed. After a while a knock sounded and, upon opening the door, Myrtle found a student with a message for her. The principal wanted to see her at his home immediately.

"Oh dear," she said. "Am I in some sort of trouble?" She racked her brain in vain for the solution as she washed her face and combed her hair before hurrying to answer the summons.

Wedding Bells

Myrtle's eyes nearly popped out of her head when she entered the principal's living room, for there sat Rossier and his father. "Whatever is Mr. Campbell doing here?" she wondered. Rossier's dad always made two trips a year to Los Angeles in order to sell his cattle. When he'd completed his business he visited his son at college, but she knew the visit wasn't due until later, when he would attend the graduation exercise. While the girl's mind puzzled over the questions that presented themselves, she managed to remember her manners and greet the visitor politely.

The principal invited her to be seated and then handed her an official-looking envelope. "Here's a letter you must read carefully," he said.

She scanned the sheet quickly. It proved to be an emergency call for Mr. and Mrs. James Rossier Campbell to work in Africa. As she read the appeal she burst into tears.

"What's the matter?" the principal asked kindly.

"But—but I'm not Mrs. Campbell yet. "I want"—sniff-sniff—"to graduate!" she sobbed. "I've worked so hard for my certificate, and then just a month or two before I finish I have to leave! Mother and Dad will be so disappointed."

"That's easily arranged." The principal smiled. "You and Rossier have both worked well, and I'm sure all your teachers will feel perfectly justified in granting you your certificates."

"But what of the final examinations?"

"What of them? Surely you're not going to complain if you don't have to take them?" he said with a smile. "My dear, experience is the best teacher, and I'll guarantee you're going to have enough experience to provide you with more practical knowledge than you could gain in any classroom. You'll graduate in absentia."

"But—but we're not married yet," Myrtle said, shaking her head.

Rossier's eyes lighted up. "We can rectify that soon."

"But you're not of age yet," Myrtle argued.

"That's where I come in," Mr. Campbell spoke up. "I was impressed to bring the cattle to town earlier than usual because God knew Rossier would need my signature so he could get married. God needs you, my children. Though I'd have chosen a field of labor nearer home, I cannot refuse when God calls on me to sacrifice my son in His service. How soon can you be ready for us to go to your home in Downey, Myrtle?"

"I could have my things packed by lights out tonight," she answered.

"Great! Then let's plan to leave around four o'clock tomorrow morning," Mr. Campbell suggested.

"I think we should have a short season of prayer for God to guide these dear young people. We'll miss them, for they've been two of our most dependable students," said the principal.

In Downey, California, where the Henrys lived,

Mother Henry called to her husband. "I need a sack of flour. I set the yeast for bread making last night without checking the flour bin. Would you be able to fetch it for me before you go out to the field?"

"I'll go right now," Mr. Henry answered, giving his wife a kiss as he walked out of the kitchen. But before he'd gone half a dozen steps he discovered he'd left his wallet in the pocket of his other trousers. "Tch, tch, tch! No use going to the store without any cash," he muttered as he retraced his steps. He hurried into the house by the back door as Myrtle, Rossier, and Mr. Campbell entered at the front.

"Mom?" Myrtle sang out as she ran down the hallway, leaving the two men standing just inside the front door.

"Myrtle, child!" her mother gasped as Myrtle flung her arms around her mother. Father stood back questioningly. Something very serious must be wrong. Whatever had happened? The parents stood there waiting for a reply. Then Myrtle burst into tears.

"Darling, darling, what's the matter?" Dad patted her shoulder reassuringly as he put his arm around her.

"It's nothing. Only—" she struggled to control her emotions, "only first you must meet Rossier and his dad."

Her parents realized suddenly that they had guests who had remained unobtrusively at the front door. They apologized for their seeming neglect.

"No apologies needed, friends. Just wait till you hear the children's story. I won't steal their thunder. Go ahead and tell them," urged Mr. Campbell.

Rossier looked at Myrtle. "Very well, I'll be the spokesman." Myrtle smiled through the tears that still were on her cheeks. "Mom and Dad, Rossier and I must get married right away."

14

The color drained from her mother's face. Her father's eyes flashed fire, and he opened his mouth to speak, but Myrtle gave him no chance.

"The General Conference has asked us to get married so we can go to Africa as soon as possible. It's an emergency."

Her mother caught her breath. The color returned slowly to her cheeks, and her dad's clenched fists relaxed.

"I believe this is a call from God," Mr. Campbell spoke solemnly. "My son could not get a marriage license, for he is underage; but God sent me along just in time so I could give my consent."

Just then Myrtle heard an impatient whimper coming from the bedroom. "Oh, I must see Mildred. I've been so busy with my own affairs I forgot all about the baby." She ran to the bedroom to pick up the baby that had been born while she was away at school. How could she go away to Africa now she had a wee sister! She'd longed to have a sister for so many years! And at last she had one. She held the small child close and carried her to the kitchen.

"I can't leave you, Mom, and Mildred—" Myrtle hugged Mildred closer. "I was going to take over all the housework so you could have a complete rest this summer. Why must my heart be torn by conflicting loyalties?"

"I know how you feel, dear. But always remember we gave you to God when you were born. God will give me the strength I need." Mother smiled bravely through misty eyes. She turned briskly to the men, almost as if ashamed of the display of emotion. "Why don't you take Mr. Campbell and fetch the flour so I can finish the bread?" she said to her husband.

"That will give Dad and Mr. Campbell a chance to

discuss farming and ranching and what have you." Myrtle smiled. "But *I'm* going to bake the bread while you, Mother, become better acquainted with your new son."

Myrtle carried baby Mildred to the bedroom and laid the little one on the bed while she changed into work clothes.

Within one week everything had to be ready for the wedding and for their departure. This Myrtle knew would be one of the busiest weeks.

Under an arch festooned with bridal wreath and calla lilies, Myrtle Henry changed her name in the presence of her family and a few close friends to Mrs. Myrtle Campbell. Since she had not met the rest of Rossier's family they decided to stop over a few days at the Campbell ranch in Arizona. All too soon the time came when the young couple had to leave for New York and the ship that would take them to Africa.

Together they stood by the ship's rail and watched the Statue of Liberty look smaller and smaller.

"Do you have a queer little empty feeling right here?" Myrtle put her small clenched fist over her heart as she asked the question in a tremulous tone.

"Yes," her young husband replied. "Not only an empty feeling, but it's sort of a sickly scared feeling too."

"As if a million butterflies inside one didn't know where they were going?" Myrtle's small hand now crept into her husband's.

They stood silent, side by side, somewhat awed by the big step they had taken.

But they stood together. They had a oneness of purpose.

Sink or Swim

When the young couple reached Cape Town on the southern tip of Africa they were disappointed to find that city almost like any in the United States. However, they soon learned that Cape Town was not their destination. They still had many miles of land travel ahead of them.

People from the division headquarters took them in for a few days. It didn't take long for them to realize that this was not America. The English spoken sounded strange to their ears. The money—pounds, shillings, and pence—they thought they would never become accustomed to, and then there was the train that their newfound friends took them to board for their trip into the interior. Their names they found posted to a section of a train coach. Fortunately, they were told, "The train is not crowded, or you might find yourselves being placed in different compartments, men in some, women in others." A long corridor ran the length of the coach, and the compartments opened onto it.

By the time they had been cooped up in the compartment for five days, Myrtle and Rossier exclaimed "at last" in unison when the conductor walked down the corridor calling "Bulawayo."

17

Quickly they gathered the few articles that they had brought with them in the compartment and were waiting for the train to screech to a halt.

The young people glanced apprehensively at each other as they stepped off the train. Would anyone be there to meet them? If not, what would be their next move?

Hardly had they stepped onto the platform when a man and woman came up to them. "Are you the Campbells?" they asked.

"We surely are," Rossier replied with a broad smile on his face. "You must be from Solusi Mission."

Myrtle took the woman's outstretched hand. "I'm glad to be on solid ground once more," she sighed. "My head is dizzy from the rocking and rattling of the train."

"I thought we'd be out in the wilds when we reached Bulawayo, but judging by the station it's almost as civilized as Cape Town." Rossier sounded rather disappointed.

"Well, Bulawayo is not the mission." Melvin Sturdevant laughed. "Have patience. Here, let me get a porter to help us with your luggage."

The young people followed the seasoned missionary as he and his wife led them along the platform and out of the station to a wagon drawn by a span of sixteen oxen! After stowing the luggage strategically around the purchases the Sturdevants had already made for the mission, the men helped the two women up into the wagon, then the two men jumped in. The African driver cracked his long whip and the oxen lumbered down the road.

The Rossier Campbells knew now that they were on the last thirty-two miles of their journey.

"How I wish we had the pillar of cloud that shaded

the Israelites. The sun is scorching me to a crisp," Myrtle ventured as the merciless heat added to the discomfort of the jolting over the bumpy road.

"I could do with some padding on this seat," Mrs. Sturdevant said with a laugh. "These wagons have no springs."

At last the sun sank lower on the horizon. Suddenly it disappeared and within minutes the stars came out twinkling, while the rising moon lighted up the ribbon of road that stretched unendingly ahead.

"Who-whooo?" an owl's eerie question broke the rhythmic creak-creak of the wagon and the plod-plod of the oxen's feet. Then a weird and drawn out "haa-ha!" sounded almost directly behind them.

Myrtle clutched Rossier's arm. "What's that?" she whispered.

Mrs. Sturdevant must have heard, for she answered the question. "That's a hyena. We do have interesting night sounds, don't we?"

Myrtle, about to reply heard a deep, threatening "ugh, ugh, ugh." The African driving the oxen cracked his whip sharply several times making a sound like rifle shots.

"That should scare away any inquisitive lions," Elder Sturdevant explained.

Owls, hyenas, now lions! Rossier held his bride a little closer. Those lions would have to get him first! He was truly thankful for the story of Daniel in the lions' den, and silently he reminded his heavenly Father of it. And surely, he thought, they must have had the same protection from the lions. The roar came no nearer. Shortly after midnight the oxen pulled the wagon into the Solusi Mission compound. The Sturdevants took the Campbells into their home, and Mrs. Sturdevant gave Rossier a candle and a box of matches and showed them to their room. It did not take the travel-weary couple long to undress, pray, and tumble into bed—but not to sleep. As they lay in their beds, they heard "krrts, krrts-krrts-krrts!"

"Please light the candle, and let's see what that queer noise is," Myrtle whispered. "Do they have rattlers in this country?"

Rossier fumbled with a match and lighted the candle. The flickering flame finally threw a distorted shadow onto the wall. Both Myrtle and Rossier climbed carefully out of bed and began to look cautiously under the furniture, in the corners, and finally under the bed. Myrtle placed one hand on the bed and pressed down as she peered under the bed. Suddenly she started to laugh. "Oh, Rossier, our mattress is made of dried corn husks which crackle loudly under the pressure of our bodies. That's what makes the strange noise every move we make." Once they knew *that*, they blew out their candle and in no time at all had drifted off to sleep.

It seemed they'd only just closed their eyes when they were awakened by voices outside. The students had come to serenade the new missionaries. Myrtle and Rossier dressed hurriedly and in the gray dawn of morning showed their faces at the window. Though they appreciated the thought, they'd have appreciated their bed even more at that early hour. They heard the Sturdevants up and about, and since they themselves were dressed, they agreed they might as well go out to see what was expected of them.

Elder Sturdevant took Rossier off to tour the mission and to introduce him to Victor Wilson, a young South African who had been at Solusi for a year. Myrtle found Mrs. Sturdevant in the kitchen busy making sandwiches.

"Good morning, my dear," Mrs. Sturdevant, looking up, said, "I hope you slept well in spite of the strange surroundings."

"Very well, thank you," Myrtle replied.

"I'm so sorry I had to use all the bread for our lunch on the train," she apologized.

Myrtle's eyes widened with the unspoken question, and her hostess hurried to explain.

"Melvin and I are leaving on vacation right after we've eaten."

Myrtle gave a little gasp. "How—how long will you be gone?"

"Three months. By the way, you can make bread?" It was more a question than a statement. When the newcomer nodded, her hostess continued. "You can make bread right after breakfast. I set the sponge last night. You have to feed J. V. (Victor Wilson's nickname). Elder Hyatt, our union conference president, is also here for a few days."

There was another little gasp, then, "You mean I have to entertain the union conference president?"

"You'll entertain even such distinguished guests as our overseas General Conference men! But don't be alarmed, for they all enjoy good cooking. Something else: I haven't had a chance to make the emblems for the ordinances tomorrow, but Obed will be able to show you where to find the ingredients. Obed, by the way, is my chief-cook-and-bottle-washer. Oh, you'd better make johnnycake for breakfast since there isn't even one slice of bread left over."

"Johnnycake? What's that?"

The woman smiled. "I forgot you wouldn't know. Johnnycake is what they call good old American cornbread in this part of the world."

Myrtle sighed.

Since Mrs. Sturdevant had finished fixing the lunch box, she bustled off to pack the last few things. Fortunately at that moment Obed, the young African, arrived. He had picked up a smattering of English, so Myrtle was able to communicate to some extent. He showed her where to find the things she needed for johnnycake; and he stoked up the fire. By the time the men came into the kitchen from their morning tour, Myrtle had ready: burned fingers, a hole burned in her new apron, a feather-light johnnycake, fried potatoes, and scrambled eggs.

Everyone did full justice to the substantial meal. Worship followed, good-byes were said to the Sturdevants, and they took off.

Myrtle had a frantic feeling as she saw the dust billow up behind the departing missionaries. She might just as well have been dumped into the middle of an icy lake and told to swim to shore—or sink. She wondered whether she'd ever make "the shore"!

Nothing for Jesus

"How does one make the emblems for the Communion service?" Myrtle wondered. "Communion Sabbath! What do I do? Obed," she asked, "what does the missionary lady do to get ready for tomorrow when they eat bread in church?" she asked.

For a second the African looked blankly at her. Then he understood. "Oh, Madam wants to know how to make the bread and wine? See, here's the little book that says what Madam must do. And here in this tin Madam will find the little black things Mama Missionary boils up for the wine."

Myrtle examined the little black things and discovered they were raisins! Obed showed her how much water to use, and pretty soon the wine was bubbling on the stove. Then she turned her attention to the little book and learned how to make the Communion wafers out of whole wheat flour, water, oil, and salt.

Now there was the bread dough to attend to. After the loaves of bread were slowly rising near the wood stove Myrtle stood in the kitchen doorway and gazed pensively outside. Suddenly she noticed a lemon tree laden with juicy fruit. Why, there were lemon trees at home! But before she could feel homesick she had the inspiration she needed. She could make two luscious lemon pies, one for lunch and one for Sabbath dessert. She fixed the pies with special care, for this would be the very first big meal she'd made for her husband.

At noon the men came in and washed up. After they had done full justice to the meal Myrtle had prepared, she brought in one of the lemon pies, which she cut into four pieces.

"M'm--I find this lemon pie has a peculiar taste!" said Elder Hyatt with a frown. Myrtle's eyes opened wide. What could have happened to his piece of pie?

"My piece tastes just fine." Rossier came to her rescue.

"Mine's delicious," complimented Mr. Wilson.

"Well, mine has a decidely more-ish taste," said the guest of honor, Elder Hyatt, with a mischievous twinkle now in his eye.

Rossier nudged his wife under the table and mouthed, "Do you have any more?"

Myrtle wanted to say, "Yes, but it's for tomorrow." However, she held her peace, went back into the pantry, and cut up the second pie, which vanished just as quickly as had the first. "At least I've made Rossier proud of my pie-making ability," she thought as she made another two pies for their Sabbath dinner.

By the time the shadows had lengthened she had everything ready. As Rossier came into the house he sniffed appreciatively. "Mmm, something smells yummy," he said as he kissed his wife. "By the way, Victor told me that you can expect to have the Sparrows here before sundown. They always spend the ordinance Sabbath here."

"Victor? The Sparrows?" she raised her eyebrows as she questioned.

"Victor—that's Mr. Wilson. The Sparrows are a South African family, maybe they're English. I don't

24

know, anyway, they are our nearest white Adventist neighbors," he explained.

Myrtle looked forward eagerly to meeting these new friends even though it meant she had to scurry around a little faster in order to have the guest room ready for them.

Sabbath morning, just after breakfast, several kinky-haired youngsters came to the back door for something. Myrtle, at a loss as to what they wanted, stood there speechless. At last she caught a word that sounded a little like "chair," but she was sure she was mistaken, for why would they want her chairs? Mr. Wilson must have heard the voices rising higher and higher, as all were getting completely frustrated. He came to see what the fuss was about.

"These children seem to want something but—" the young missionary lifted her hands helplessly.

A smile creased his face. "They want your dining-room chairs, Mrs. Campbell."

"Whatever for? I thought I heard 'chairs,' but I was sure I'd misunderstood."

"Come in and get the chairs," he told the children in the vernacular. They marched off triumphantly, chairs on their heads, and Victor Wilson explained, "We'll sit on them at church."

"Why can't we use the church pews? I don't like the idea of discriminating that way," Myrtle argued in her innocence.

"You'll soon change your mind," he answered laconically.

"That I will *not*," she replied under her breath.

A little later Myrtle discovered that Mr. Wilson was oh so right. A pew consisted of a pole supported on either end by a couple of bricks. It looked anything but inviting, and she shuddered at the thought of having to sit through Sabbath School and church on those precarious, backless perches. Thanks to the children the missionaries had comfortable chairs up on the rostrum. Fortunately the Africans were completely satisfied with their seats, which were so much better than what they had at home.

As she walked up the center aisle of the church with Mrs. Sparrow, Myrtle noticed several large baskets below the pulpit. "What are those things for?" she whispered to Mrs. Sparrow.

"Those are for the offerings."

"Offerings? Those huge things?"

The older woman nodded. "People don't have much cash, so they bring ears of corn, sweet potatoes, even live chickens—see, there's a woman bringing an egg!"

"But—but?" Myrtle still mystified, questioned her friend.

"Tomorrow the deacons will sell all the produce, and that money will go toward the Sabbath School offering."

"Oh!" A light dawned.

"These dear people have so little, but they want to sacrifice for Jesus!"

Then Myrtle's eyes went back to the "pews." How thankful she was that she didn't have to balance herself on those poles. Then she smiled as something else struck her. "Say, aren't there any complete families in this church? None of the men have wives, and none of the women have husbands!"

Mrs. Sparrow smiled. "It's the African custom that the men and boys sit on one side of the church while the women, girls, and small children sit on the other."

"Hmm! I'm glad it's not necessary for *us* to follow that custom."

Just then the Sabbth School officers filed onto the

rostrum, so she sat back to listen attentively.

And that was the moment four ambitious teenagers decided to make their entrance into the church. Dressed in some very strange costumes, they stalked up the center aisle and swaggered to seats on the very front row—no doubt so the new missionaries would be sure to see them in their finery and be duly impressed. Unfortunately they were so intent on creating an impression that they failed to sit down with the necessary caution. The seat rolled from under them, their feet shot into the air, and they landed on the laps of those behind them. It was the funniest thing Myrtle had ever seen. Not a smile creased the faces of the Africans, but it certainly caught Myrtle off guard, and she knew she was going to disgrace her husband. Quickly she slipped out by a side door, and there she laughed till it hurt. Each time she succeeded in straightening her face she would imagine those boys upended and she began to giggle afresh.

"Now then, Myrtle Henry—oops, I'm not Myrtle Henry any longer," she soliloquized. "I'm acting like a frivolous teenager. Remember you're a married woman," she said to herself. But all her reasoning didn't help as she pictured those boys strutting up the aisle, past the basket of produce. Those boys had walked right past those baskets without dropping in anything for Jesus, not even a handful of corn. They'd been so busy trying to impress the missionaries that they'd forgotten all about the Master. Suddenly she had no more desire to giggle. "Do we, who should know so much more, treat Him the same way?" With that sobering thought she went back to her seat.

Green Tomatoes

On Sunday Rossier took Myrtle around and showed her the mission compound as Victor Wilson had done for him on Friday. The students were hard at work hoeing weeds out of the acres of corn. Bulawayo has a ready market for the school's produce. And the students worked hard to get that produce ready.

"Here's where you'll start your teaching career, my sweet schoolmarm," Rossier teased, as he took Myrtle to a small thatch-roofed building.

Myrtle blinked and swallowed. It surely didn't look like even the most primitive country schoolhouse back home in California. She wondered how she'd manage. And then she thought of something else. She remembered the confusion Sabbath morning when the children wanted the chairs. "But, Rossier, how will I communicate with my students?" she asked.

At that moment Victor Wilson, who had heard the question from another room in the school, answered it for her. "Don't worry about that. Most of the children speak only Sendebele, the language of this area. You'll have a good translator."

Myrtle shook her head. She wasn't so sure that she'd be able to use a translator, but at any rate she would do her best!

Monday morning the young teacher found that Mr. Wilson had been quite correct about the translator being very capable. The man who helped her did an excellent job—at least as far as she could judge. He hardly hesitated as he told the children what she said. As she left the classroom that afternoon the African beamed. "Ah, Madam, I am happy to be helping you, for I am learning many new things myself. You make the work so very plain."

Myrtle felt amply repaid for the effort she had put into preparing the lessons for the day. Strange though, no girls attended the classes. The boys were so anxious to learn! And how they could memorize the Bible! Later on she found that at night they went home and taught their parents most of what they'd learned in school that day.

Both Myrtle and Rossier worked hard at learning the Sendebele language. It came easy to Rossier, but with Myrtle it was another matter. Perhaps it was because her interests were so divided. Not only did she have to teach, but she had to look after the home. It seemed that each time she sat down to concentrate on Sendebele, something came up to interrupt her.

Three months passed by quickly. When the Sturdevants returned to the mission, the Campells moved into a smaller cottage. They didn't have much furniture, but at least it was *their* very first home. And Myrtle had no end of ideas. She used one of their steamer trunks as a table, and when she draped a snowy tablecloth over it, it looked quite attractive, but it wasn't very comfortable for them to sit at the table, for there was no place for their knees. They had no chairs, but several kerosene boxes from their local store they used for chairs until the day they invited Elder Hyatt to lunch. He sat right down on one of the

29

kerosene boxes that had a nail sticking up. He tore a hole in his trousers. That did the trick.

"Why, my dear young lady, you can't use these paraffin (kerosene) boxes as chairs. Just see what this nail did to my trousers! Tomorrow you're going to Bulawayo with me, and we'll buy you a decent table and six chairs to match," he announced as he looked ruefully at his trouser leg.

"Oh, Elder Hyatt, I'm so sorry about your trousers. Give them to me and I'll mend them," Myrtle offered.

The president wasn't too sure that such a young missionary would be able to do a really neat job on his trousers, but since he wished to wear them on the train when he went back home the next day, he changed into his Sabbath trousers and gave her the torn pair.

After a few minutes Myrtle returned the trousers to him. "Well, my dear, you certainly are an accomplished seamstress. I'll wager my wife won't find the tear until she comes to press my suit for me," he complimented her when he looked at the place she had neatly mended.

How thrilled Myrtle felt as she set the table—not the steamer trunk—that first evening when the new table and chairs graced their dining room. "Doesn't Mama's silverware look beautiful on this lovely table?" she asked Rossier ecstatically.

"It surely does. I really appreciate Mother Henry's giving us such fine cutlery, especially since it's an heirloom," Rossier agreed.

Though they grew plenty of food such as peas, beans, corn, sweet potatoes, and peanuts, for some unknown reason nobody on the mission bothered to grow other vegetables. The newcomers felt starved for lettuce and cabbage and other "real garden stuff," as Myrtle put it, so when someone went to Bulawayo, her "town list" was headed by the word *SEEDS*. Rossier helped her fix three boxes which he filled with dirt. Then she planted her seeds the way her dad had done back home, watered them tenderly, and waited impatiently for results. Surely nothing tasted quite as good as those first little radishes. The hard work she'd put into them enhanced their flavor many times. Unfortunately the beetles seemed to think this new breed of missionaries had nothing to do but produce a garden just for their benefit. Since that was definitely not her intention, Myrtle finally beat them to it by making little tents around her lettuce plants, so that they, instead of the bugs, could feast. The tomatoes matured much more slowly than the rest of the vegetables. As she gazed at the little green fruits, her mouth watered for the ripe, red tomatoes she hoped to reap. Being pregnant, she also thought of the vitamins those tomatoes would supply her.

One afternoon Myrtle had company. While she and her friend chatted happily about knitting, sewing, and baby clothes, the visitor's two little girls ran outside to play. The two women were still exchanging recipes and pattern ideas when their conversation was interrupted as the children dashed into the house.

"Look, Mama, see what we finded. Aren't they 'bootiful'? " they shouted excitedly and emptied the contents of their little Dutch aprons—Myrtle's precious green tomatoes.

Myrtle could not restrain her groan of horror, and the mother, realizing that her hostess was very much upset, said soothingly. "Never mind, Myrtle, I'll give you the recipe so you can make delectable green tomato preserve."

Myrtle knew all about green tomato preserve. She didn't want *green tomato preserve*; she wanted fresh ripe tomatoes to tickle her jaded palate. But there was no use crying over spilled milk, or maybe one should say stripped tomato plants. So she tried to hide her disappointment, though she was sure she'd never longed for any food as much as she did for those tomatoes. She almost wept when she looked at those poor, denuded plants without one tiny little fruit left on the vines.

As Myrtle recounted the episode to Rossier when they were in bed that evening she sniffled, "I want fresh, ripe tomatoes. They are far too expensive in Bulawayo for us to even look in their direction, yet Dad has acres—maybe that is a bit exaggerated, but he does have fields of tomato plants back home. Why can't I have some tomatoes too?"

"There, there, dear, you're just wrought up. Tomorrow you'll be able to laugh at the experience," her husband soothed.

"I won't laugh, not tomorrow, or the next day or—" Then seeing his distress at her outburst she spoke more calmly, "I guess I'm just tired. School has been rather trying the last few days. Sometimes I wonder whether I'm accomplishing anything with the youngsters. Are they getting to know Jesus, or am I just teaching them to count, to read and write?"

"I'm sure some of the children are learning to love the Master, but let me ask you, Do all the children in our schools back home become Christians?"

Myrtle's face brightened. "Of course some do, and some don't. I guess it's the same over here. I suppose—" but Rossier's gentle snores told her it was no use telling him what she supposed!

Little-No-Good-Thing
and the Mamba

Little-No-Good-Thing could only be described as a spoiled brat, a completely spoiled African brat. Her mother had had five, six children, or was it seven? But all had lived only a month or two. Because Mother and Father were heathen, they thought the spirits were envious of their good fortune in having so many lovely babies and so had snatched them away in early infancy. When Mother and Father had one more child, father decided to outwit the spirits. He called her Little-No-Good-Thing in the hope that the spirits would think she wasn't worth bothering with. To his delight his ruse seemed to work, for the baby lived and grew and developed into a sturdy child. The parents were so thankful Little-No-Good-Thing had survived the first hazardous years that they denied her nothing. Whatever she wanted, the child got. African children were required to help around their homes, but not Little-No-Good-Thing. She was in a fair way to growing up lazy, selfish, utterly worthless. And then the father died.

"Since Father died we have no money with which to pay our taxes or to buy clothes," Mother said. "I will have to go to the city to find work," she told Little-No-Good-Thing as they ate their cornmeal mush one evening.

33

"Goody!" The child clapped her hands. "I've always wanted to go to Bulawayo." Her eyes sparkled in anticipation.

"I'm sorry to disappoint you, but you are not going with me. I must go alone," her mother told her.

"No, I want to go too, Mama," Little-No-Good-Thing insisted. "I will scream very hard if you do not take me," she threatened.

Her mother shook her head. "I cannot take you, my child. I will have to work for a white madam, and I know the white madam does not want little girls running along behind their mothers."

"I will not run along behind you. I will walk around in the city."

But for once her mother was adamant, and no amount of argument or fuming changed her mind.

Early the next morning mother and child put their worldly possessions—sleeping mats, blankets, and mother's aluminum cooking pot—in baskets on their heads and set off toward Grandmother's house. After several hours they reached their destination.

"My, how Little-No-Good-Thing has grown," the old woman said after they had exchanged the usual greetings. "So you are going to work in the city!" Grandmother said to the child's mother, "You will have to be very careful, for I hear tell Bulawayo is a bad place. But I shall be happy to have a strong girl to help me."

Early the next morning Mother set off for Bulawayo. That very morning Grandmother told Little-No-Good-Thing to make herself a broom so she could sweep the yard around their hut.

"I don't want to sweep. I want to play," announced Little-No-Good-Thing, and the corners of the child's mouth turned down.

"After you have swept you may play," the old woman insisted.

Much against her will the girl picked a few twigs and swept around the house. She grumbled continually, and the poor job she did matched her grouchy attitude. Later in the day Grandmother sent the girl to fetch a clay pot of water from the stream, half a mile away. The child liked this task no better than she did the sweeping. All Little-No-Good-Thing wanted to do was eat and play, so it seemed that Grandmother was continually commanding and scolding.

One weekend Mother came home for a visit. "See, I have brought both of you presents," she told her family. "Here's a cloth for your head, Old One," and she gave Grandmother a bright colored bandana, "and here's a dress that my madam's children used to wear." She handed her daughter a white cotton dress with sprigs of forget-me-nots and daisies adding splashes of color. Both Grandmother and Little-No-Good-Thing thanked Mother for the gifts. Then the child said, "What is it like in the big city? Can I go back with you?"

"No, you can't go back with me. Instead I want you to go to the school near here. If I could read and write I could earn much more money. You are going to learn. See, here is a shilling to give the teacher. Next time I come I'll bring more money."

Grandmother shook her head. "Nonsense! The child does not need school. If she goes she will learn many things that will make the spirits angry with us. See, I've never been to school and I'm content."

For once Grandmother and Little-No-Good-Thing agreed, but Mother insisted. The last thing she said as she left Sunday afternoon was, "Now mind. You are to go to school tomorrow!"

Grandmother had much to say about education in general and teachers in particular. "I've heard that the teacher has a big stick, and if you dare to move, he whacks you with it. If you cannot say the things he writes, he whacks you. Oh, school is a dreadful place. But your mother is so foolish. She says you must go, so I'll take you. That school will make you more lazy and good-for-nothing than ever. Why did I have such a foolish daughter?" And the old woman sighed heavily.

Monday afternoon Grandmother had to almost drag the unwilling child to the grass-roofed mission school in their vicinity. The child's eyes darted furtively around the room in search of the big stick. She decided the teacher must have hidden it very carefully, for she could not see it anywhere. At first she was scared as a gazelle penned in a cage, but gradually she relaxed as the teacher told the children stories of One called Jesus and taught them songs to sing and words to read off the chart on the wall. Not once did he bring out the big stick, even when the students made mistakes in their work. By the time school was dismissed Little-No-Good-Thing had decided she just might like "being educated."

But Grandmother did not share the child's enthusiasm. "Just wait. That teacher has been to the big school where the white man has taught him many tricks. He'll whip you when you least expect it," she threatened darkly.

But each day proved to be as good as, or better, than the last, or so it seemed to Little-No-Good-Thing; and the best part of the day was when the teacher told them about Mr. Jesus who loved them all. Little-No-Good-Thing began to love this Jesus too. And as she loved this Jesus, she became more and more happy. Instead of grousing when asked to do a chore, she eagerly helped the old woman. In fact, she even thought of doing extra tasks to lighten her grandmother's load. Happy songs replaced her grumbling. Grandmother could not fail to notice the change, but it did not please her. She suspected that her grandchild was becoming a Christian, and she feared the evil spirits would curse them if that should happen. When the girl knelt by her pallet to pray, the old woman scolded and shouted so loudly that she drowned the words. At last Little-No-Good-Thing decided to find herself a spot in the forest where she could pray in peace.

After she had looked around for a while, the child found a large spreading umbrellalike tree that suited her. She cleaned away the thorns and pebbles so she had a smooth place on which to kneel. Every day she went to her favorite spot and told her troubles to the One who is ever ready to listen. Always she asked her heavenly Father to change the old grandmother's heart so she, too, could know the joy of being a Christian.

One afternoon Grandmother had been particularly abusive, and the child knelt quietly awhile before beginning to pray. Suddenly she stiffened. Her heart missed a beat, for there, slithering determinedly toward her she saw the biggest, ugliest black mamba she had ever seen. She did not need anyone to tell her that the black mamba is one of Africa's deadliest snakes. Her prayer froze on her lips. She stared terrified at the evil creature. Its forked tongue flickered rapidly as if it was licking its lips in anticipation. The beady eyes tried to hypnotize her as they did some luckless bird. She didn't dare move even her lips. But she remembered that her teacher had said that you didn't have to mouth your words, for Mr. Jesus was so wonderful He could even see into your thoughts. Silently she prayed, "Help, Mr. Jesus, help!" The mamba came closer,

closer, then passed not a foot distant, to lose itself in the forest behind her. She jumped to her feet and, with the speed of a scared impala, she dashed home, not stopping till she dropped to her knees in her own doorway. "Thank You, thank You, Mr. Jesus," she repeated over and over.

"The child has gone crazy. I knew that education was no good," the old grandmother exclaimed as she ran around the hut to see what had caused the commotion.

"No, no, I'm not crazy. A black mamba came at me, and Mr. Jesus saved me. I was just thanking Him," said the child as she stood up.

"Impossible! Whoever heard of a black mamba not attacking!" Grandmother stared at her grandchild.

"It's true! I asked Mr. Jesus to save me and He did," the girl exulted.

Grandmother weighed the important matter. "Do you think I could get Him to help me like that? The spirits would never help anyone that way. He might be better than the spirits."

"My Mr. Jesus wouldn't help you, because you don't know Him." Little-No-Good-Thing spoke with authority.

"Very good; tomorrow I will go to the school with you, so I can get to know Him."

True to her word Grandmother accompanied the little dark-skinned missionary to school the next day. But she wasn't quite sure, so she accosted the teacher: "How do you *know* that your Mr. Jesus is stronger than the spirits? Who told you that?"

"Ah, Old Woman, the missionaries at Solusi told me, but they also taught me to read. So I have proved all these things for myself," he answered gravely.

"Very well, get me a Black Book and teach this child

to read it. I will pay you when my daughter comes from Bulawayo,'' the old woman commanded.

Grandmother had no more objections to Little-No-Good-Thing learning about Jesus; and as the child learned she, in turn, taught the woman. Together they were baptized, and Little-No-Good-Thing changed her name to Marita (Martha), the one who works.

If only Myrtle could have gone out into the bush to see the change Christ had made in those lives, she would have been completely satisfied that it was indeed worthwhile to be a missionary—even if some missionaries had to long in vain for ripe tomatoes!

Marching Orders

Rossier was doing very well at learning Sendebele, and though Myrtle could not twist her tongue around the foreign sounds, her ears were beginning to adjust to them so that she was able to understand something of what her students were saying. Both Rossier and Myrtle felt as if they were settling nicely into their niche at Solusi, and then came a most upsetting message. A young couple at a station to the north had both come down with malaria, and it was feared their baby boy might also become infected with it because the mission was in a mosquito-infested area. That was bad enough, but because of their seeming susceptibility to the disease, their station director felt they should get out of that area. The Campbells were asked to change places with them.

Since Myrtle expected their first baby very shortly, she and Rossier were advised to stay in a hotel in Bulawayo until they could travel farther. To save money they took a room so they could fix their own meals.

One evening as they returned from a day in a nearby park they passed a house where it was obvious the folk were frying onions for supper. "Doesn't that smell yummy?" Myrtle asked.

"It surely does. Let's fix onions for ourselves tonight."

Myrtle fixed a whole panful of onions, and she certainly ate her share of them. Toward midnight she awoke.

"I'm afraid I was too greedy this evening," she groaned. "Those onions are fighting in my tummy. I'd better take some medicine." She got out of bed quickly.

"My poor darling! Is there anything I can do?" Rossier asked. "We don't want you ill now, while we're away from home."

The medicine didn't help, and after an hour Myrtle knew she could not blame the onions for her discomfort. She was in labor. "Rossier, you'd better fetch the midwife," she told him.

Rossier pulled his trousers over his pajamas, stuck his feet into his shoes—fortunately into the right ones, for he was so excited he wasn't responsible for his actions—and set off at a trot. He covered the half mile to the nurse's home in record time and then tried to get her to emulate his speed on the way back.

"Now, now, Mr. Campbell, don't get excited. This is your first baby, so there's no need to rush like this," the nurse tried to reason with him. However, to be on the safe side the good lady stepped up her pace. And it was just as well she did, for less than half an hour after she walked into the room Baby Vivienne Mae informed the world that she wasn't too pleased with the change of surroundings.

Ten days later the Campbell family, three in number now, started on the train journey to Rusangu Mission in Zambia.

"Oh, look, Rossier, see these people alongside the tracks? They look just like the pictures in mission storybooks. Oh! Oh! See that anthill. And the trees. This is the real thing," Myrtle exclaimed ecstatically as she gazed out on the changing scenery that seemed to unroll before their eyes as the train chugged and wheezed its way along. Rossier, busy with the grammar of the new language they would be using at the new mission, hardly acknowledged Myrtle's delight. He only grunted and went on with his study. When the conductor rattled the lock of the compartment door, Myrtle opened it slightly.

"Good evening, madam; evening, sir." The conductor smiled at the couple.

Rossier fumbled in his wallet for the tickets.

"No, I don't need your tickets," the conductor said. "I've just come to tell you that your mission director has asked that we put you down at the point on the line nearest to Rusangu. If we took you to the nearest station, you'd have an oxcart trip of several hours to your destination. The mission folk will have a bonfire by the side of the track where you are to get off. I'll be along to help you when it is time to get off." And with that he backed out of the compartment, shutting the door as he left.

Toward midnight the conductor returned.

The couple awoke with a start when the conductor rattled the door and called to them. Shortly afterward the train jolted to a stop. Myrtle and Rossier pressed their noses against the window and looked out into the darkness. The track was built along a ridge, and by the light from a bonfire they noticed it seemed a long way down to where the mission director stood waiting. The conductor, true to his word, helped them get their luggage down to the man so far below. Then Rossier jumped down, and Myrtle handed the baby to the conductor who very carefully lowered her to her waiting papa who passed her to the waiting mission director. Then Rossier reached up and took Myrtle's hand, and she jumped lightly down. She breathed a sigh of relief as she took the baby from the mission director and held her wee one close. They turned and waved to the conductor and to the engineer, who had been an interested spectator. The latter blew the whistle, and with a mighty jerk the engine belched a cloud of steam, and the train was on its way.

Elder Anderson, the mission director, introduced himself. The Campbells learned that Elder Anderson's wife had died of blackwater fever, a complication of malaria fever in which the red corpuscles are killed and passed out by the kidneys, thus turning the "water" black. He seemed happy to share his home with the Campbells.

But at last Myrtle and Rossier and the wee baby moved into their own home. Of course it was necessary to have servants to do the housework. They also needed money in order to pay their taxes. Therefore, Myrtle had to carry a full teaching load. However, she never left the care of her baby to servants. Instead she took a homemade playpen and a blanket to the schoolhouse and set it in a corner near her desk. While the baby cooed and played with her toys in the playpen, Myrtle taught the African youngsters the three R's—Reading, 'Riting and 'Rithmetic—as well as Bible and singing. Myrtle loved her work. All was going well until Rossier broke the shattering news that he had to go on safari.

"You'll have to fix supplies for several weeks. I'll be out in the bush with no chance of buying anything," he told his wife.

"What do you mean?" she asked.

"The schools out in the bush have to be inspected at

least once a year, so Elder Anderson suggested I get the job done before the rainy season sets in."

"How long will you be gone?" Myrtle frowned.

"A month!"

"Rossier!" Myrtle wailed, "A whole month! How will I manage without you? Why, we haven't been separated for even one night since we were married!"

"Don't you ever fear," Rossier tried to reassure his wife. "You'll do just fine, for the Lord will be right here by you."

Myrtle and Rossier packed clothes, bedding, food, medicine, and ammunition into boxes to be carried on the heads of African porters. After Rossier committed his wife and baby into the care of their heavenly Father, he kissed them, then hurried down the path to catch up with the carriers.

Now came long, lonely days for Myrtle, the only white person on the mission, Elder Anderson, having gone back on furlough to the United States. The Africans came to her when they needed anything, and fortunately there were several Solusi graduates at Rusangu who could speak English. They were a great help, but the days seemed very long.

One evening Baby Vivienne seemed particularly fussy. No sooner would Myrtle lay her down in her crib than she would whimper. "I wonder why she doesn't go to sleep; she's usually such a good baby," she muttered as she picked the child up once more. Myrtle noticed her flushed cheeks, so she touched her forehead lightly. "She doesn't feel too warm to me, but I'd better check with the thermometer." The thermometer proved that the baby had a fairly high fever.

"But why didn't I feel it? I'll take my own temperature," Myrtle told herself, placing the thermometer in her own mouth. "Of all things. No wonder she did not seem warm to me; my temperature is just as high as hers. What can I do? If only we had a doctor near us!" Panic seized her for a moment.

Since there was no doctor, Myrtle did the next best thing—she wrote Rossier all about her troubles. But then she remembered he was far beyond the reach of the postal service. In desperation she sent for one of the teachers, a young Solusi graduate who knew English.

"Madam looks ill," he said when he saw the woman's flushed face.

"Yes, Teacher, I am ill," Myrtle said. "But it's my baby that worries me."

"Please, Madam, we must do something about the baby. Can you not write our director about the baby?"

"I *have* written my husband, but I don't know how to send my letter to him," and she lifted her shoulders and spread her hands in a helpless gesture.

"Oh, that is easy. I will find a porter and he can carry the letter for you. But do you know where he is?"

"He left me his itinerary." Myrtle seeing the teacher shake his head and a bewildered look on his face, realized that the big word had stumped him. "He left me the names of the places he was going to visit," she explained, holding out the itinerary to him. "He should be right here for a day or two," and she pointed to the name of a place on the list.

"Very good, I'll give your letter to a student and send him off immediately," the teacher said as he took the letter.

The carrier reached Rossier the next day and found him also ill with malaria. But when he read his wife's

45

letter, he immediately dressed, and with two of his trusty porters set off for home. Surely those were the longest sixty miles he'd ever traveled. He hardly stopped to eat or drink till he reached home the following day. His feet were blistered and bleeding, and his fever was even higher than that of his wife or baby. Myrtle put him to bed immediately and gave him the best care she could. By evening he had much improved. Realizing his wife's condition had worsened, he put her to bed and gave her some of the same treatments she'd given him.

One interminable day after another dragged by with first Rossier down and Myrtle up, then Myrtle down and Rossier up. However, both of them worried continually about Baby Vivienne. At last after a week they all began to improve.

"Myrtle, darling, I hate to say this, but I believe you and Vivienne ought to get out of this malaria-infested area," Rossier spoke deliberately.

"Rossier, I can't. My place is by your side." Myrtle shook her head vehemently.

"No, Myrtle, it's your duty to look after Vivienne and the new baby we are expecting. Delivery at the Cape will be much better than here at the mission. Since I have to open a new school near the Zambezi River, I'll be on safari much of the time. Vivienne is not snapping out of this attack. At the Cape you'll both get strong." He ended the discussion with a kiss.

Once the decision had been reached it didn't take them long to get ready for the long train ride to the Cape. When the day of departure arrived, Myrtle leaned far out of the window to watch the solitary figure on the platform grow ever smaller. When the train rounded a curve, she could see her husband no longer and drew back into the compartment.

"Now let's settle our things, my baby," she told Vivienne, who cooed and gurgled as the train jiggled her back and forth. Myrtle hoisted the luggage onto the rack above her head. "But-but where's *your* suitcase?" she gasped. Vivienne's only answer was to blow bubbles at her mommy. Frantically Myrtle opened first one suitcase, then the other. It was no use—the baby's things had been forgotten on the platform or someplace else. At any rate they were not in the compartment! What a time Myrtle had. Every evening she washed out the baby's clothes and draped them around the compartment to dry. By the time they reached Kimberley the baby's clothes looked much the worse for wear. Fortunately Myrtle had time to buy a few things for Vivienne to wear while in Kimberley, where they had to change trains.

During Myrtle's stay at the Cape, Vivienne grew stronger and happily received the new baby sister, Marguerite, when she arrived. By the time Myrtle was ready to take the train back to Zambia, Vivienne had had her third birthday and eagerly helped care for her six-month-old baby sister.

"See, Vivienne, we're getting hear home," Myrtle told her little daughter as the train rattled over the rails through the forests of Zambia. The train stopped at a siding, then jerked on its way once more. Suddenly the compartment door opened, and Myrtle looked up expecting to see the conductor. "Rossier!" she exclaimed and flew into his arms.

"And now meet the newest member of our family and her big sister." Myrtle presented him with the new baby and pulled Vivienne from the seat where she huddled somewhat shyly.

He bent to embrace the little girls, but they shrank back from this stranger. Vivienne didn't know her

47

daddy any longer—eight months is an eternity when you're only two-and-a-bit. Besides Rossier had grown a mustache and beard. To the two little girls he appeared strange and rather fierce.

Myrtle gathered them close and told them, "That's your papa."

From the shelter of her arms they peeped at him, but didn't want any closer acquaintance. It took several days for the strangeness to wear off. But one day Vivienne crawled up onto his lap and baby Marguerite reached out and pulled his mustache and beard when he bent over her crib.

"Birdies Bite!"

Myrtle found things somewhat different when they reached the mission. Elder Anderson had returned, and with him had come a new wife to mother his little girl. Mrs. Anderson had a delicious meal ready for the Campbells when they drove into the station, a meal that tasted very special by comparison with the food Myrtle and Vivienne had eaten on the train.

How good it felt to be back home again! Sometimes Myrtle would wake to the distant roar of a lion, but that didn't scare her. She'd learned that only the boldest man-eaters would enter an African compound, and there were not too many man-eaters around. What really frightened her, though, was the high-pitched whine of the little mosquito. She had developed a healthy respect for the mosquito and the malaria germs it so often carried. During the dry season they had little to worry about, but when the rains came, then there would be the malaria-carrying mosquito to fear.

Vivienne seemed to thrive on the mission. She talked to the flowers and the birds, her dolls, and anyone who happened to be passing. She never wandered far from the backdoor, and her mother checked on her periodically. However, Myrtle told the child many times as she pointed to a corner of the yard, "You must not go near that white box in the corner of the garden. There are bees living in that box, and the bees will sting you.''

"What are bees, Mommy?'' Vivienne had asked, and Myrtle had explained.

"Those little insects that you see going in and out of that hole in the box are bees.'' Myrtle had taken Vivienne by the hand and led her a little closer to the box. "Now remember, stay away from that box,'' Mother warned.

And Vivienne did stay away from the box—at first. But that beehive seemed to have magnetic powers. Each day she went just a little closer. One Friday when her mother was particularly busy Vivienne wandered out into the yard. Her feet seemed to be irresistibly drawn toward the forbidden box. Before long she sat down in front of the hive to watch the busy little workers.

"Birdies, pretty birdies,'' she repeated over and over.

Suddenly she decided she wanted to hold the "birdies,'' and when a bee alighted on the projecting platform and Vivienne saw her chance, she stretched out her hand and grabbed it. Ah, it was hers.

But as suddenly as her small hand grabbed the bee, it jabbed deep into her tender finger. Surprised at the sudden sharp jab, she opened her mouth to scream. That seemed to electrify a dozen bees that were leaving the hive, and they attacked simultaneously.

"Mommy, Mommy! Birdies bite!'' Vivienne screamed louder than before.

Myrtle, who had been changing the beds for Sabbath, suddenly heard "Birdies bite!'' She ran to the window. Though she could not see Vivienne she could hear the anguished cry and saw a swarm of bees milling around. Guessing what had happened, she snatched up a bedsheet off the floor and ran outside and around the house. There sat her little girl attacked by a swarm of angry bees. It took but a moment to reach the child, envelop her in the sheet, dash back to the kitchen and slam the door to keep the swarm out of the house.

"Father, help me!" Mother breathed as she removed the sheet and picked the vicious insects off the child's arms and legs.

"Run down to the compound and call the master," Myrtle shouted to her kitchen helper.

The young man fairly flew down the road to the place where Rossier was helping the Africans sack dried corn. "Master, Master, the Mama Missionary is frightened. The child is all covered with bees. You must come quick," the young man panted.

Rossier knew he could not run as quickly as the African, so he instructed him, "Go, tell Mama Missionary I will come as quickly as I can."

The young man turned and sped back up the hill like the wind. "Mama, the master is coming! The master is coming. But Mama must give to the child much, much milk," he instructed.

"Milk?" Myrtle looked up puzzled, but knowing something needed to be done for the little one, she decided milk could do no harm. "Put the milk in a cup for me, please," Myrtle told the man. She held the cup to the child's lips. "Drink the milk, darling," she commanded Vivienne.

Obediently Vivienne gulped down the liquid. It was no sooner down than it came right up, all over Myrtle, herself, and the floor. She was on the point of getting the child to drink a second glass of milk when Rossier stepped in.

"Praise the Lord!" he exclaimed.

"What?" Myrtle exclaimed.

"Yes indeed, praise the Lord. So many stings, so much poison—why she could easily have died," Rossier said when he saw the red bumps and welts all over the little arms and legs. The poison in a beesting is the same as that of a rattler's bite! We need Divine help with this emergency."

Together Myrtle, Rossier, and Myrtle's young helper knelt and asked their heavenly Father to bless their efforts for the little girl. Though Vivienne was a very miserable little one for the best part of a week, she finally recovered, much wiser for the experience. Nothing could tempt her near the hive. She'd had enough of the "birdies that bite."

Blackwater Fever

The following Friday afternoon when Rossier returned to the house from sacking corn, he said wearily, "I'll get my bath and then go right to bed."

"I'll follow suit, for I'm about worn to a frazzle with looking after Vivienne," Myrtle agreed.

It didn't take Rossier long to get to bed. Shortly after putting her little ones to sleep she walked into their bedroom and found her husband writhing with pain. She did what she could to alleviate his agony, but nothing seemed to help.

"I'm going to fetch Elder Anderson. Maybe he'll know what to do; he's had so much experience," Myrtle told her husband as she ran out of the house into the darkness without her shoes. Usually she hesitated to walk out of the house in the dark for fear of stepping on a puff adder, but she hadn't even thought of snakes.

"Please, Elder Anderson," Myrtle gasped as Elder Anderson came to the door. "Come and help me. Rossier is very ill. He is burning with fever, and his urine is pitch black. Please come quickly."

"His urine is black?" he asked. "Go back quickly. Heat bricks. Heat water. I'll be right over," and he turned into the house to dress.

There was no need to heat water, for Myrtle always

had a four-gallon kerosine can of water on the wood stove, and the cook always left the firebox stoked before he went home in the evening. But she did heat four bricks.

"What is this dreaded blackwater fever?" Myrtle asked the seasoned missionary as they worked together over her sick husband. "I remember you telling us something about it before but—"

"It's a complication of malaria. The red blood cells sort of deteriorate and are carried off by the kidneys. Thus the sick person passes 'black water.' I lost my first wife with it."

Myrtle noticed his eyes misted as he remembered. "But why is it so dangerous?" she asked.

"Because if too many of the red cells are destroyed there is nothing to carry the oxygen to the various organs, and the patient virtually suffocates. That's why you have to keep your husband very quiet and warm so his oxygen needs are as low as possible. Now you go and rest and I'll stay by him. Remember you have the two little girls you must care for."

"May we have prayer first?" Myrtle asked.

"Assuredly," Elder Anderson answered.

So the two of them knelt by Rossier's bed and pleaded with the heavenly Physician to bless their efforts.

Sleep eluded Myrtle, for her thoughts were anything but tranquil. True, she had committed her dear one to the Father's care, but what if it was His will to lay him to rest? Should she try to carry on alone? Should she go back to California to her dad, who was finding it very hard to adjust to life without her mother, who had recently fallen asleep in Jesus? At last she fell into a fitful sleep.

It was easier to be optimistic when the sun chased the night away. She kept a careful watch over her husband throughout the day. Continually she lifted her heart in prayer. For eleven long, wearisome days and nights Myrtle did not remove her clothes save to bathe and change into clean things. At times she held a slate over the patient's mouth. The mist on the slate proved that Rossier was still alive, for she could find no pulse. At the end of eleven days, all seemed futile. Rossier slept for seven hours. Myrtle's courage hit rock bottom. And then, even as she watched and prayed, he opened his eyes and in a weak, tremulous voice said just one word, "Myrtle!"

"Oh, Rossier, my love!" She fell on her knees. Tears of relief and joy coursed down her cheeks.

He smiled gently at her as much as to say, "Now, don't you worry; everything's going to be fine."

Day by day he grew stronger—more like his old self. But it was almost a month before he could stand alone long enough to be weighed on the farm scales. He had lost fifty-two pounds. His clothes hung on him like bags.

"I look like a scarecrow," he said as he made fun of himself.

"Well, Marguerite and Vivienne aren't scared by the lack of flesh on your bones. Scarecrow or no scarecrow, I praise God for the miracle that I still have a husband. But I surely don't want another such frightening experience," Myrtle responded.

"I, too, thank the Lord for your recovery," Elder Anderson told his young colleague. "But you must not stay longer at Rusangu." He recommended that the Campbells be moved to a more healthful area. And not long afterward they received a call to locate in the Switzerland of South Africa, the lovely mountainous country of Lesotho.

Mantea's Baby

The Campbells had just settled in their new mission home. The two little girls, wide-eyed with wonder at all the new sights and sounds, scampered around the mission yard.

Myrtle, although used to mission life by now, had to learn new ways and new customs of another tribe of people. She longed to help these people learn a better way of life and to help them know Jesus.

Not long after their arrival in the Lesotho country, Rossier had to go on safari, visiting missions and schools in the area. Myrtle and the two little girls stayed at home.

Up in the hills, not far from the mission, lived Chief Pulyanani with his wife and small child. Chief Pulyanani's people were not Christians, but the chief had seen many of the wonderful things the Christian missionaries had done for his people.

Now his child was sick.

His wife, Mantea, held the little one in her arms as she sat on the dirt floor of their hut and rocked the child back and forth, trying to soothe it.

Suddenly her voice rose to a loud wail of anguish. "Our baby is about to die."

"No, no. In the morning the girl will be better," and

the chief prepared to settle himself on his mat once more.

"Not so," his wife insisted. "Three of my babies have died, and now this latest one is going to die as well." Once more her wail pierced the stillness of the night.

"Tomorrow I will fetch the Missionary Mama, and she will make our baby well," he promised.

Mantea shook her head. "No Mama Missionary can get this devil out of my little one."

"Oh, yes, this Missionary Mama can. I have seen her pull the devil out of a man's mouth just like this," and he demonstrated vigorously. "She sat on the man's chest while two helpers held him down, then she stuck a shiny thing into his mouth and pulled the devil right out of his head."

The woman's eyes opened wide. "Really?"

"Well, the Missionary Mama didn't actually *sit* on his chest, but she did get the devil out. I saw the devil all bloody, hanging onto the tooth in the shiny thing." He nodded wisely.

"Then go! Fetch the Missionary Mama *now*," the young mother commanded.

"Tomorrow—" the man stalled.

"No, now," she insisted.

Pulyanani sighed. He shook his head, wondering at the way of women. He stood up and stretched, wrapped his blanket tightly around himself, picked up his stout stick, and walked over to the beer pot bubbling merrily near the fire. He bent and took several long sips from the long, hollow straw which extended beyond the rim of the clay vessel. The beer should give him the strength and fortitude to hurry down the mountain in the moonlight, the time when evil spirits were abroad, he told himself.

Myrtle Campbell sat up with a start. Who could be pounding on her door at that time of night? Was it a drunk African? Was it a thief? But surely a thief would try to enter as quietly as possible. Maybe she'd had a nightmare; but no, there was that loud bang-bang again. She slipped out of bed and pattered barefooted across the cement floor to the window. "Who is there?" she called softly.

"Pulyanani, Chief Pulyanani! Mama Missionary, you come quick." The man outside sounded urgent.

Myrtle hesitated. She was alone with her two little girls. "Dear Father, protect us," she breathed as she went to the door and opened it a crack. She could see a tall African. Pulyanani—Pulyanani—ah, she remembered, Rossier had spoken of the man. He was the paramount chief in the area, a real dyed-in-the-wool heathen.

"What is the matter, Chief?" Myrtle asked.

"It is my baby. She is like to die. You must come and pull the devil out of her," he pleaded.

"Can it not wait till morning?" she asked.

"No," he shook his head vigorously. "No, now. The devil very strong. Come now!"

Myrtle could smell alcohol on the man's breath, but she answered, "Very well. Wait for me a minute," and she shut the door.

The hurricane lantern that she lighted threw grotesque shadows about the room as she dressed hurriedly. Then she went to the beds where her girls lay sleeping. Quickly, she breathed a prayer, picked up the light, and joined the chief.

Up, up, up the narrow mountain trail Myrtle hurried, hard on the heels of the man. She huffed and puffed with every step. "I'm not much of a mountain goat. But maybe I'll lose an ounce or two," she consoled herself with a wry smile in the darkness.

At last they reached the chief's kraal (cluster of huts). Myrtle had to get down on her hands and knees in order to crawl through the low, tunnellike opening into the house where Mantea still moaned softly over her babe.

"Where is your wife?" Myrtle asked as she looked around for the baby's mother.

"There," and Pulyanani pointed to Mantea.

Myrtle shook her head. Poor child-wife, to have so much responsibility while still so young! She turned her attention to the task in hand as she reached for the baby.

Mantea watched the woman's face anxiously for some glimmer of encouragement. Myrtle hid her shock when she removed the filthy cloth in which the infant was wrapped. How the little one stank! It was clearly a case of severe dysentery. "I surely wish I were a doctor or at least a nurse instead of a teacher," Myrtle muttered as she handed back the pitiful bundle to the mother.

"Aren't you going to pull any devils out of the baby?" the disapppointed father asked.

"No, not yet. I must go down to my house to fetch medicine and other things. You make some water hot, and I will come back quickly. But first let us pray. Kneel down, fold your hands, close your eyes," and Myrtle demonstrated. Then she prayed a simple prayer of faith that God would bless her efforts and heal the baby. She left, and hurried, stumbling and sliding, down the mountain. At home she saw her own two little ones were still sleeping quietly, so she gathered up a bucket, soap, towels, clean diapers, a clean bottle, nipple, and some milk. "But what can I give the little one to stop the diarrhea?" she murmured. Then a smile lighted her face. "I'll try some flour and water like my mother used on my brothers and sister, and I'll flavor it with peppermint to make it smell like medicine," she told herself.

Back at Pulyanani and Mantea's hut, Myrtle took the babe from its mother. Mantea watched anxiously as the white hands washed the skeleton that was her precious baby. The wee one had shriveled into scarcely more than a shadow during the four or five days she had been so ill. When Myrtle cradled the clean baby in her arms, she opened the tiny mouth and stuck the nipple between the lips. It gulped the food as if famished, but Myrtle would not give it very much at one time.

"There, Mama Mantea, take your baby. I'll be back later with more food and medicine," she promised as she handed the drowsy infant to its mother.

"But where is the devil?" the father asked anxiously.

"Ah, my God took the devil out when we prayed and your eyes were closed," the quick-witted woman replied. "You can see for yourself; now the child is sleeping quietly."

God blessed Myrtle's efforts. He rebuked the enemy, and like a wilting flower revives after a rain, so the baby came back from the very gates of the grave, and in an incredibly short time she was a gurgling bundle of joy.

Mantea, grateful to the missionary for her help, came with the baby the next Sabbath to the little church in the valley. Here she learned about the God to whom the Mama Missionary had prayed.

"Aiye, Pastor, I like the God you told us about today. I'll be back to hear more next Seventh day," she assured the African preacher as she shook his hand at the church door.

Happiness Is . . .

"Now, then, Mantea, it was all very well to take notice of the Mama Missionary and her church when the baby was ill. But now she is well we do not need to go back to the church," Pulyanani scolded peevishly when Mantea returned from services the second Sabbath.

"But I am so very thankful—" the woman began.

"That's why I did not mind it when you attended church the first time. But there's no sense in going any longer." The man spoke with a tone of finality that ended all discussion.

However, he had not changed Mantea's mind. She liked the God she'd heard about at the Seventh-day Adventist church, and she intended to find out more about Him. Sabbath morning she hurried down the mountain again. Myrtle's heart sang as she saw the fruits of her labors for the Master. Mantea smiled back at the white woman and *her* heart rejoiced too, for she sensed the Mama Missionary's love. Sabbath School and church fulfilled all Mantea's expectations.

"Aiye, Pastor, that was a good story [sermon] you had today," Mantea told the African preacher.

"Good. Come back next week, and you'll hear more," the man replied as he shook her hand warmly.

"I will. And every Sabbath after that, for I want to be a Seven-days woman."

Mantea was still within earshot of the church when she met Pulyanani. "You no-good wife!" Pulyanani shouted. "I told you not to come back to this church."

"Stop screaming at me! You're drunk, Pulyanani," Mantea spoke quietly, almost soothingly; but it only infuriated her husband more.

"Do you dare to criticize Pulyanani, Chief Pulyanani?" With that he lashed at her with the *sjambok*, a hippo-hide whip.

His attack took the woman completely by surprise as the whip snaked around her bare ankles. She gathered up her long skirt and dashed away from her husband, but not before he'd succeeded in striking her now-exposed legs. He tried to follow her and she heard the whip zing through the air, but she was beyond his reach. He struggled to catch up with her, but he was no match for her younger sturdier legs. His free use of beer and tobacco told their own tale, and he was soon winded. Mantea reached her hut, hurried inside, and shut the door. But she need not have worried, for Pulyanani went to the hut of one of his other wives to show his displeasure still further.

The next Sabbath Mantea arrived at the church before anyone else, for she was determined Pulyanani would not prevent her from attending. But although he was not able to keep her home, he was waiting for her outside the church after the service. Once more he managed to hit her legs several times before she got away from him. Several of the lashes on that first Sabbath had become open sores. She had treated the wounds as best she knew how, and by this Sabbath the scabs were almost ready to come off. But when the man hit her again the wounds went deeper. It became a weekly performance, except that each Sabbath her legs were in worse shape than the week before.

One morning Mantea shook her head as she looked at her now-swollen, raw legs. "I won't be able to walk down the mountain next week. I cannot let Pulyanani beat me again. I'll have to ask my Jesus to help me," she muttered. And so she prayed.

Early the next day Mantea heard a commotion near her hut. She listened and learned that Pulyanani was going to a government meeting for all the chiefs. This was her opportunity! As soon as she was sure the chief had left, she slipped out of her hut. With the baby asleep on her back and a pot of food on her head, she hurried down the mountain. She knew she could not take refuge at the mission, for Pulyanani would be sure to look there for her. And if the missionaries defied him he could cause much trouble. Instead she set out for Ficksburg, a small town in South Africa. She had never been out of her own area, but a fear of Pulyanani gave her the necessary courage and determination to try to escape his persecution. She had eaten the last of her food when she came to a lone farmhouse. The farmer, busy with his animals, looked up as she approached.

"Please, Master, can you help me?" Mantea asked in the vernacular.

Fortunately for her, the Dutch farmer spoke her language. "What is the trouble?" he asked gently.

Before she knew it, Mantea had told the whole story. "And so Chief Pulyanani won't let me be a Seven-days woman," she ended.

The man smiled. "Our God led you to the right person, for I'm a Seven-days man myself. I'll be glad to help you. Come to my wife. She can use someone to work for her. You can live in that hut over there." He pointed to a round hut not far from the big house.

The farmer's wife received Mantea kindly. "You look hungry. Here's some food left over from our dinner. Take it to your house. After you have eaten, come back and we will talk," she suggested knowing that Africans do not care to eat in front of strangers.

When Mantea came back to the kitchen Mrs. van Zyl asked, "Can you cook? Can you wash and iron?"

Mantea shook her head.

"No, well, I'll teach you. But you cannot work wrapped in a blanket. Here's a dress of mine that should fit you. And some clothes for your baby. Tie the little one to your back with this cloth. The master has told me all about you, and we have decided that you can help me with the housework. We will feed and clothe you and give you a little money as well."

And so began a new life for Mantea. On Sabbath she accompanied Mr. and Mrs. van Zyl to the church in Ficksburg. At first Mantea was overcome by all the sights and sounds in the city, which was really just a small town in a farming community. Days slipped into weeks, and the weeks became months. Mantea felt contented.

Pulyanani was not content, however. When he returned from the government meetings he'd forgotten his annoyance at Mantea and went straight to her hut. He found the door shut, and he called to her to let him in. When there was no response he looked more closely and found the door had been latched on the outside. Inside the hut he found no sign of Mantea or the baby. He asked each wife in turn where Mantea could be, but no one knew anything. He hurried to the mission, and even there no one had seen her. Mantea had vanished. Months went by with no news of his wife and child. Then one day a friend told him that he had seen Mantea coming out of the Seven-days Church at

Ficksburg one Saturday morning.

Mounted on his sturdy pony, Pulyanani started off for Ficksburg. On Sabbath morning he waited in the vicinity of the Adventist church. At noon the congregation came out of the church, but they stood around chatting. They were all white except for one black woman. That had to be his wife.

Pulyanani watched eagerly so he could catch her as she walked away alone, but his plans went sadly awry, for Mantea was whisked off by a white man and woman. Pulyanani determined not to lose her so easily. He dug his heels into the sides of his pony and followed as fast as he could to the home of the white couple who had taken his wife.

Mantea, busy changing out of her church dress, heard a deep voice calling, "Mantea, Mantea!" Surely she was mistaken. She opened the door and there stood Pulyanani. She was going to call for help when the man silenced her as he pleaded, "Mantea, you are my favorite wife. How could you go and leave me like that?"

The woman took a breath to answer, but he hurried on. "Come home with me, and I'll buy you a beautiful new blanket to wear."

"I don't need a new blanket. See my dresses and my baby's dresses." She waved to the clothes hanging in a rough cupboard behind her.

"Ah, I'll buy you a new cooking pot and lots of food."

"I don't need a pot, for I eat what I cook for the master and his wife. See how big and strong the white man's food has made my baby!"

Pulyanani noticed the chubby little girl peeping from behind her mother. His mouth dropped open. "Is *that* our baby that nearly died?"

5—A.D.

Mantea nodded. "See what I mean? I have a nice house, fine clothes, good food; I go to church each week, and the master gives me a penny for Sabbath School and a penny for church. *You* beat me when I went to church. You never gave me any offerings."

"Please, Mantea, I will never beat you again. You may go to church each week. I will give you two pennies for church. Surely it is better to live like an African than like the white man." Pulyanani thought he saw signs of her weakening and he hastened to press his point. "And I'll tell you what. I'll let you and the girl ride my pony, and I'll walk by your side. What African woman has had that privilege? You'll be the envy of all my other wives, in fact of every woman in Lesotho!"

That clinched the matter.

"But we cannot leave today, for it is God's Sabbath. I will go and tell the master. Maybe you can stay here tonight and they'll give you some food. These people are true Christian people. Tomorrow I will go home with you," his wife promised.

Mrs. van Zyl was sorry to see Mantea leave, for she had been a faithful worker. "But I am glad you will be back with your husband; God wants families to be together," the woman encouraged Mantea.

It had been an interesting, peaceful experience, living with the white folk, but the cluster of huts belonging to Pulyanani on the mountain was home to Mantea.

Pulyanani, heathen though he was, kept most of his promises to his favorite wife. She attended church without fear of punishment, and he gave her two pennies for her offering almost every week. He even accompanied her occasionally, but he would not join the church. When the African pastor added his voice to Mantea's plea, he shook his head sadly as he confessed: "It is too late. The beer pot won't let me go!"

Those around Mantea could not fail to be impressed by the joy she radiated. Soon the other wives begged her to tell them her secret source of happiness.

"It's Yesu, Master Yesu," she told them.

It wasn't long till the five heathen wives of Pulyanani joined Mantea at church each week. Soon all of them were preparing for baptism.

As Myrtle Campbell watched the six joyful, black faces smiling at her Sabbath after Sabbath her own heart rejoiced that God had given her a chance to labor with Him. "Thank You, God, for calling me to be a Missionary Mama," she whispered as the congregation sang, "Praise God, From Whom All Blessings Flow."

Why, Lord?

"We talk of the Seventh-day Adventist movement; well, dear, the accent is definitely on the *movement*," Rossier announced one day.

"What do you mean?" Myrtle looked questioningly at her husband.

"We're being asked to move—"

"Not *again*!" Myrtle remonstrated. She couldn't help being just a trifle upset.

And so they moved. This time to Johannesburg, sometimes called the golden city because it is the center of the gold mining industry. But it didn't seem like a golden city to Myrtle, for there was no church-operated school in that area. However, Myrtle decided they would send their girls to Spion Kop (the forerunner of Helderberg College) that took in students from the lower grades through college. Of course this was going to be expensive, but since she was an excellent seamstress she did dressmaking to bring in the money necessary for the school fees and transportation.

Even though she never complained about missing her youngsters, Rossier guessed her feelings. One day he announced, "Say, I have a suggestion. I have to make a field trip to the Natal Coast to open up work among the Asians living there. I believe the railway is advertising half-price excursions for Easter. Why don't you and Lois (for by now another daughter had come to gladden the family) come with me as far as Ladysmith, and then you can spend the time at our Spion Kop School with the girls?"

"Oh, Daddy!" Lois flung herself at her dad, and Myrtle wasn't far behind.

Of course they made the girls a huge boxful of goodies, for it seems boarding school students are always famished. They all had a wonderful time together, but the week seemed far too short for Mother and the girls.

As Mother and Lois left Spion Kop and started back to town, the weather appeared to sympathize with their feelings. The heavens opened up, "the rain came down and the floods came up," and the vehicle in which they rode had a dreadful time in the sticky, muddy morass that was supposed to be a road. Although they'd started in plenty of time, that downpour held them back just long enough for them to reach the station minutes after the train had departed, and they had a tiresome wait for the next one.

As they sat on the hard bench in the uninviting station, Lois became increasingly bored and restless. Finally she exploded, "You know, Mommy, I don't see why Jesus didn't keep that rain away for three hours or so. After all we're missionaries, and He might have done that for us."

"Hush, Lois, we are not to question God's dealings," her mother reprimanded gently.

"Yes, but—" Lois was not convinced.

At last the next train arrived, and then they found out why they'd missed their connection. The first train had been involved in a serious wreck, and many of the passengers were dead or maimed.

"Oh, Mommy, what if we hadn't gotten stuck in the mud? Maybe we'd have been one of those who are now dead." Lois hid her face in her hands as if to blot out the image her fertile imagination had painted.

"Indeed, yes, we could very easily have been a statistic," Myrtle agreed.

The child shuddered. "And to think I kind of blamed Jesus when all the time He was planning for us in love!"

"Yes, dear, we're all like that. When things go wrong, we feel God doesn't care. Let's try to remember this the next time something unpleasant happens."

"Do you mean you also get such feelings?" Lois looked as if she could not believe her ears—to think *her mother* could have such negative thoughts—that was almost preposterous!

Myrtle sighed. "That's true. Many times we've had things happen that we couldn't understand, but through the years I've come to realize that though we may not see any good reason for the disappointments that come our way, someday God will make it all plain."

"Just like that hymn you taught us," Lois interrupted.

"Yes, dear. So we can daily develop our faith." Mother nodded.

At that moment the conductor arrived and their conversation ended. The rest of the journey was uneventful and almost before they knew it they were home, and their trip to Spion Kop remained a delightful memory.

White Hands, Black Feet

Usually when Rossier went on safari Myrtle stayed home. However while he held an institute for the workers in Zululand it was decided that she should teach the women to sew and knit, how to cook nutritious meals with the food on hand, and how to care for their babies. That meant they would go to Zululand together.

At the end of the first day of the institute, as they were preparing for bed, Myrtle's words tumbled out excitedly. "Oh, Rossier, this is thrilling! These dear women are so very anxious to learn. I wish I had the gift of tongues like you do. But at least I can say Hello to them. I'm surely glad I learned that greeting at Spion Kop. I felt a bit rusty with it at first, but after I'd greeted each of the women, it rolled out quite smoothly. And what I lack in words, I make up for by smiling."

"How's your translator doing?"

"I think he's doing well. Of course I don't know what he's saying, but he's quite fluent, and the women all nod as he talks, so I presume they are agreeing with what I'm saying!"

As Rossier came in for supper one evening he exuded an air of suppressed excitement.

"Something happened," Myrtle challenged.

He shook his head incredulously. "You're uncanny; you know me so well. You have a new name, my dear."

"What's so exciting about *that*?" Myrtle asked in disgust.

"Because I like your new name! You know the Africans usually name a person after some special characteristic they see in them. The women call you The-Mama-Who-Smiles. Now isn't that a name to get excited about? But that's not all. Today the Zulu queen sent for me. Although she's been a Seventh-day Adventist for some time and has partaken of the Lord's Supper, she's never joined in the Ordinance of Humility. Now she has expressed the wish to do so with *you*."

"With *me*? When?" Myrtle's eyes opened wide.

"Since we won't be here over Sabbath I agreed we could have the service at the royal hut tomorrow."

Myrtle took a deep breath. "Whew! What a responsibility is mine—to represent our Master correctly."

"No need to worry. He's there to help you every step of the way," her husband consoled.

The queen's house was larger but still very much like the round, mud-walled, grass-roofed huts of her subjects. It, too, had no windows, and only one low door. Nearly all the African customs that Westerners consider strange have a very sensible origin. "I wouldn't want to be an enemy trying to enter the royal hut," Myrtle thought as she got down low and almost crawled into the royal domain. She remembered the time she'd gone to help Mantea. Her visit then had proved such a blessing. How she hoped this visit would be just as productive.

In the center of the room, on the floor, a fire burned,

more to give light than heat, for Zululand has a semitropical climate so is never very cold. She thought of the verse, "Now we see through a glass, darkly." Indeed they did see each other "darkly." Myrtle, however, was at a greater disadvantage, for it was more difficult to see the chocolate-colored woman in that flickering glimmer than it was to see Myrtle's white face. But they saw enough so they could serve each other. And there was no difficulty in seeing the queen's radiant smile of inner joy at following Christ's express command. Although neither could speak the other's tongue, they were both satisfied. The love of Christ binds hearts together irrespective of the color of the skin or the difference in language and culture.

Famine

Once again the Campells were moved, this time to Gitwe, Rwanda, the home of the tall Watusi as well as the short, almost pigmy Datwa. Life promised to be more exciting than ever.

Gardening time in Rwanda always intensified at the end of the camp-meeting session. Women hoed gardens and planted the seeds. Soon tiny green shoots appeared. The dry season would soon give way to the rains. But the first year the Campbells were at Rwanda things didn't work out that way. The women prepared the soil and planted the seed, but the rains did not come. There were no noisy thunderstorms. The tiny shoots that sprang up shriveled up and died. Soon there was no food anywhere. People walked along the road searching for something to eat, but they'd be so weak they had to sit down, and where they sat, they died. The gaunt specter of famine stalked merciless through the once-lovely land.

The government brought in truckloads of food and appointed centers to care for the starving. The Seventh-day Adventist missionaries had charge in the Gitwe area. They cooked the food in huge two hundred liter (fifty gallon) gasoline drums that had been cleaned thoroughly. People from the surrounding hills lined up to receive their portion, but because there was never enough to go around the missionaries had to examine each person. "You—you had food yesterday. You still have enough strength to come back tomorrow, so you cannot get anything today. This person here won't last twenty-four hours without help, we'll give him food today." The missionaries had to make the hard decision.

As Myrtle helped out at the food kitchen she noticed two emaciated little girls who came all alone for a handout.

"*Mwalimu* [teacher], where are the parents of these children?" Myrtle asked.

"Ah, *Madami* [Madam], their parents are dead. Their family—they not want them because the family say not enough food for own childs [children]." The young teacher shook his head. "Ah, this famine, it make every person bad, same like animal."

Myrtle could not put the two little girls out of her mind. Their pinched faces haunted her dreams. The next morning she knew what she had to do. When Rossier came for his breakfast she asked his assistance.

"I must help those children I told you about last night. Won't you build me a little room—just a hut would do—behind our house?"

"No, dear, a hut behind our house would be unsightly."

His wife opened her mouth to remonstrate, to tell him *she* didn't mind if it *did* look unsightly, but he held up his hand. "Give me a chance. I can't let you build a shack, but I can get a *fundi* [qualified workman] to build a neat brick room for you." He smiled at the delighted expression on his wife's face.

Rossier didn't let the grass grow under his feet when he had a project on hand. That very morning a bricklayer came, and in a short time Myrtle had a neat "house" complete with a raised brick bed for her girls. When they came for food sometime later, with the help of an interpreter, she told them she wanted them to come to live on the mission with her—to be her girls! How she wished she could understand their excited reply, but she could understand the pleasure reflected on their faces.

Myrtle gave them a cake of soap and had them bathe themselves before they put on the dresses she'd made them. Then she let them see themselves in her mirror. They giggled as they saw their reflections in the mirror. This was more than they could ever have dreamed possible. At first when Myrtle filled their plates with food, they wolfed it down, as if afraid someone might steal it from them. Gradually their fears subsided, and they began to act like little humans.

Language presented a barrier, but love overcomes all obstacles, and soon Tamare and Madida were able to understand Myrtle's faltering attempts at Kinyarwanda (the language of Rwanda), for she was an expert at making signs to illustrate her meaning. She taught the girls how to sweep and dust, make beds, wash dishes, and prepare the vegetables for the kitchen. She showed them how to sew and knit, and they became proficient in both arts.

About the same time Tamare and Madida came to the mission, a little old man came so weak he practically crawled on hands and knees to the feeding station. Myrtle fixed him a bed on the garage floor and fed him three times a day instead of only once. Usually the Rwandese eat only one meal a day, in the evening. Tomasi, or Tom, as she called him, soon regained his strength, so she took him on as one of her workers, and he brought wood and water to the kitchen. Every Sabbath he walked up the tree-lined road to the church. He joined the baptismal class and proudly announced that now he belonged to the mission! But one day a relative appeared and persuaded Tom to go off with him.

"Oh, Rossier, Tom has gone!" Two big tears rolled down Myrtle's cheeks as she told her husband what had happened. "Do you think he'll live up to the light he received while he stayed here with us?"

Rossier drew a long breath. "That's hard to say, Myrtle. He can't read. If he goes to live near an Adventist school, though, there's a good chance that he'll go to church. We can at least pray for him."

"Why is Satan so active? I wish he'd forget about us here on the mission." Myrtle sighed.

"I'm afraid that's a vain wish. Satan is out to cause God—and us—as much grief as possible." Rossier shook his head sadly.

The Worst and the Best

When the *mwalimu* told Myrtle that the famine brought out the worst in people, he was only half right. True, the bad people grew worse, but the good people grew better, kinder, more unselfish.

There was the case of Korita and her mother during the faminetime. Korita kept begging for food.

"*Tchecheka* [keep quiet]!" the girl's mother whispered. "We must be thankful for what we get. I know one *ibijumba* [sweet potato] is not enough to fill you, but remember that everything we eat belongs to your dead father's brother."

And so Korita went to bed with a gnawing pain in her stomach. The next morning Uncle spoke the words Mother had been dreading. "I am sorry, Dina-Rosa, but you and Korita will have to go and look for your own food. You can see I have barely enough for my own family," and the man shrugged helplessly.

"You have been kind to feed us for such a long time, but where can we go now?" The widow shook her head.

"Go to Gitwe. They say the missionaries are feeding the hungry," her brother-in-law advised.

With all their worldly possessions—their sleeping mats, blankets and a battered, smoke-blackened aluminum kettle—on their heads and stout sticks in their hands, mother and daughter set out to find Gitwe. All day they walked, up one hill, then down into the valley and up another hill, on and on, and still there was no sign of Gitwe Mission. The shadows lengthened. The child was tired, hungry, and very thirsty. The sun set, a ball of fire, behind the western hills. Half an hour later it was dark, and the soft moonbeams threw weird shadows across their path.

"Look, Mama, there's a mission, up on the hill. See the church? Perhaps it's Gitwe," the child spoke with the excited optimism of youth.

"I don't think that is Gitwe, but maybe since it's a mission, the *mwalimu* will give us food."

The thought of possible food energized the child. Just then they heard in the distance "Haa-ha," the crazy bark of a lone hyena. Then from another direction came the answering "Haa-ha" of its mate. The sounds spurred both mother and child to hasten up the hill toward safety. At last they were right at the door. Korita peeped through a knothole.

"Mama, there's a lamp on the table and a man sitting at the table with a *huge* dish of *ibijumba* in front of him. Surely he'll give us some. Cough, Mama, cough!" Korita whispered.

Ahem! Ahem! Dina-Rosa coughed. The man at the table looked. Dina-Rosa was about to turn away when she heard the spine-chilling "Haa-ha" again. She coughed more loudly, since a Rwandese (a native of Rwanda) seldom knocks. With an impatient movement the man pushed his chair back from the table and came to the door and opened it a crack.

"*Urashakiki*? [What do you want?] he asked roughly.

"Please, Bwana, we are very hungry and we need a

place to stay tonight—'' the woman began. Korita pressed forward so she could smell the delightful aroma of the baked sweet potatoes.

"I have nothing for you. This is a time of famine." The man banged the door and latched it.

Two big tears rolled down Korita's dusty little face.

"Come, child, let us lie down under that bush over there. The hyenas will soon smell us, and then our troubles will be over quickly."

"*Oja* [No], Mama, *oja*! See, over there, on the next hill, there's another house. Let us go there. Perhaps those people will help us," the child begged. She grabbed her mother's hand and urged her forward.

At last they reached the top of the next hill. Again they approached the door, but even more diffidently. Dina-Rosa, a proud woman, hated to beg. Korita peered through a crack in the door. "There's a man, and a woman, and two children. They have a candle on the table. There's some food in a dish. I think it is *amashaza* [peas]," she told her mother.

The woman at the table turned. "I think I hear someone at the door. See who it is, Eliya."

The man got up and opened the door. "*Urahsakiki*?" he asked.

Just then the hyenas howled again.

"Come inside, friends,"said the man as he pulled the child into the house. "You must not be outside when the hyenas are prowling in a pack. What is your problem?" He looked searchingly at Dina-Rosa. "You are a stranger here?"

"*Yego*, Bwana [Yes, Mister]!" Soon she'd told their story. "If you can just give me a place to sleep—" she began.

"Come and share our meal," invited his wife.

"I don't need any food, if you could spare just a little

80

for Korita," the mother begged.

"Of course we have food for Korita and for you too. We were just ready to eat. You three children can stand round the table, and you can sit right here," the man invited Dina-Rosa.

After the man had thanked God for the food, a new experience for his visitors, who had to be shown what to do during prayer, Sara divided the food so each had a portion. When they were through with the meal the man had worship with them. Then he suggested: "Now, if you don't mind, you two can sleep in the kitchen behind our house. It is a safe building with a sturdy door."

"*Asante sana*," Dina-Rosa thanked the man in Swahili.

When they had wished one another Good night, Eliya took the two visitors out to the kitchen. The light from the fire in the center of the room made it possible for them to see to roll out their sleeping mats.

"Ah, Mama, this is good. Let the hyenas howl," Korita murmured as she drifted off to dreamland.

In the morning Dina-Rosa learned that their host was a teacher for the Seventh-day Adventist mission. Eliya and his kind wife insisted that Dina-Rosa and Korita make their home with them.

"Gitwe is very far, and the hyenas will get you before you reach the mission. You can sleep in the kitchen until the students and I can build you a house. You can help Sara hoe our garden when the rains finally come. And when school starts next week Korita can be one of my pupils," teacher Eliya told Dina-Rosa.

One day as Dina-Rosa collected firewood a well-dressed man approached her. "I see you have a little girl, Mama. Send her to my school. I give all my new students a piece of cloth to wear and a cake of soap so

81

they can keep themselves clean."

"That is fine, Bwana. Where is your school?" the woman asked.

"Across the valley over on that hill over there. See what a large school it is. It's much better than the school that Bwana Eliya teaches. And I have had a much better education than he had, so I'm a much better teacher."

Dina-Rosa looked at the man more closely. "I seem to think I've seen you before," she said.

"You're mistaken, for I haven't seen you," he answered.

"Your memory is not very good, Bwana. You've forgotten, but I have a good memory. My child and I came to you one dark night when the hyenas were hunting. We were starving and frightened and you—you had a dish of steaming *ibijumba* big enough to feed four people, but you coudn't spare even one *ibijumba* for a hungry little girl. *Mwalimu* Eliya has a family, but he had room for two more mouths at his table. He may not be able to give Korita a cloth or a cake of soap, his *eshuli* [school] may not be as big as your school; he may not have had a very good education, but he's given us a glimpse of One, Bwana Yesu. His heart is bigger than this whole hill! Korita is enrolled in his *eshuli*, and one day we hope to be baptized into his church," and with that Dina-Rosa turned on her heel and strode back to her house while Eliya's rival retired to his own hill like a whipped dog.

That evening Dina-Rosa told her friends of her encounter with the teacher from across the valley. After telling of the encounter she sat quiet a moment, then asked, "What I don't understand is, Why were you willing to share the little you had with us two strangers? Why were you willing to make such a sacrifice?"

Teacher Eliya thought a while. "It's like this," he said. "The *Bazunga* [white people] sacrificed to come here to tell me *Bwana Yesu* sacrificed everything in order that I might live. So I'm happy to make my little sacrifice to help show His love to others."

Dina-Rosa nodded. "*Yego* [Yes], I suppose that is what your religion is all about. I want that love that will sacrifice everything for Bwana Yesu."

Black Magic and Precious Diamonds

Many Africans sacrifice by living for Jesus. Others are prepared to die for Him, and who's to say which ones make the greater sacrifice!

During a camp-meeting safari near Bigobo north of Lubumbashi, Zaire, Rossier made a call one Sabbath morning for all those who wanted to know more about Jesus to come forward. A young girl, Kimpayi responded. After that Kimpayi gave her old father no peace till he permitted her to attend the mission school out in the bush. There she learned to know and love Jesus supremely.

Old Kikongo, Kimpayi's father, sat in the shade of his hut, his back against the wall, while he smoked his long, dirty clay pipe. He expected the arrival any minute of his crony, Tembu, who was coming to discuss a very important matter—the final arrangements for his marriage to Kimpayi, the daughter of the house. Kikongo needed to collect a little dowry, for he had had to pay out dowry to other men three times in order to get wives for his three sons. Now it was his turn to get a dowry from someone else. Kimpayi, a fine girl, good-looking, strong, and able to hoe large gardens for her husband, had an added asset. She had been to the mission school, where she had learned many valuable arts such as sewing, knitting, and cooking. Yes, she should fetch the maximum dowry from any man, particularly from such a toothless, unprepossessing old thing as Tembu. Tembu had nothing to boast about; in fact, when one considered that he already had two wives, he should be made to pay more than usual for a pretty girl like his Kimpayi. As a result of his cogitations, Kikongo decided to charge a double dowry for his daughter.

The prospective groom arrived with a loud, "*Jambo. Habari gani* [Good day. How are you]?"

"*Jambo! Habari mzuri* [Good day! I'm fine]!" Kikongo replied. "Take a seat by me," he invited, patting the ground next to him.

Tembu sat down, pulled out his pipe, stuffed it with dried tobacco leaves, and puffed away in silence for a few minutes.

"Well, you know what I have come about, of course?" Tembu began. "How much do you want for the girl? I have been thinking about the deal considerably since last I visited you. Of course you realize that I am really doing you a favor by taking the girl off your hands. You will need to make the dowry a low one because of all the inconvenience I'll have to put up with when I marry your daughter."

"Whatever do you mean?" Kikongo fumed. "On the contrary, I think you should pay me a larger dowry than usual. After all, you are an ugly old man. You have two other wives. And Kimpayi is a very talented girl." The father ticked off the items on his clawlike, dirty fingers. "Good looking, strong, able to hoe and plant your gardens, young, talented."

"Talented? Nonsense. Don't you realize that since she has been to that mission school she is far less use to me than any other girl would be? She now has fads and fancies. She will probably not want to make beer for me. And, and—she—" he paused and then went on. "There are doubtless many other things that she will refuse to do. No. Few other men would be willing to take her to wife, so you should be prepared to give her to me for a good price," argued Tembu.

"Who says that she will refuse to make beer for you? I know she is supposed to be a Christian, but we can soon get that notion out of her head. Just you leave her to me." Kimpayi's father tapped his pipe on the ground as he spoke and then stuffed it with more dried tobacco leaves.

"Good, if you can succeed in knocking that nonsense out of her head then I may be ready to pay the usual dowry: three hoes and five pots of beer—but I will not pay any more than that." Tembu wagged a gnarled finger at Kikongo.

"You ought to give me six pots of beer because she is young and strong," Kikongo argued.

"Perhaps I will give you six pots of beer, if you get her to forget that rubbish she has learned at that school. So do your best." With that, Tembu slouched off through the forest.

Kimpayi, in the meantime, had returned from class and had overheard a part of the conversation. Horror filled her heart. Was her father going to marry her off to that evil old man who already had two wives as old and as ugly as himself? Surely she had misunderstood him. As soon as Tembu left she went to Kikongo.

"*Dada* [Father]," she began, "you are very friendly with Tembu these days. I did not know you liked him so well."

"What nonsense! He is one of my best friends," her father answered with simulated indignation. "Indeed, he has been here to ask me for you, and I have just agreed that you will marry him," he said with an air of finality.

Kimpayi's hand flew up to her mouth. "Oh, no, surely not. Please do not ask me to marry that man. Why, you know that I have been to the mission school. My new religion does not permit me to marry a heathen. He already has two wives. I can't marry that old man. But even though he is so old and ugly, I would still obey you and marry him, but I *cannot* marry a heathen," she said firmly.

"Cannot marry a heathen? Indeed you *can* and you *will*. Tomorrow he is bringing me the first installment on the dowry, so you had better make up your mind that you are going to be a good wife to him." Kikongo shook his pipe at his daughter.

"No, no, NO. I'll *never* marry him," she cried.

With a snort of rage the father grabbed a supple stick and beat the girl unmercifully, shouting curses as he did so. "You'll learn to obey me, you will. Just you forget all that nonsense you have been learning. I always knew it would be a bad thing for me if I let you attend that miserable school. What does a girl want with an education! You are just as much my property as my shirt. My shirt cannot refuse me. If I wish to tear it in shreds—that is my business. And if I wish you to marry Tembu, you will do just that. You had better plan to be an obedient wife to him!" By this time his fury had spent itself, so he threw her, like a limp rag, into a corner of the hut with the parting shot: "The sooner I send you to him, the sooner you will be cured of all these foolish notions."

Next day Kikongo again broached the subject of the marriage in the hopes that the whipping had had the desired effect upon the girl. But she was adamant. She would not marry the heathen. Unfortunately for him, the girl had enough education to know that the government would not permit a marriage if both parties were not in agreement over the matter. He would have to force her to consent to the marriage if he wanted that dowry. For several days Kikongo worked on her, trying every means in his power to break her spirit, but all in vain. He could threaten, cajole, punish, but Kimpayi remained firm. She would rather die than violate her conscience. At last in desperation, he decided to visit the local witch doctor for help. Of course that would mean a present, but it would be worth his while in the long run.

"*Odi? Odi?* [Are you there?]" he called as he approached the honorable one's hut.

After a pause, back came the answer: "Yes, who wants me? I am busy with the gods, but if the matter is urgent, I can come to you."

"I need your assistance. I am Kikongo. I have brought you a chicken for the gods, if you will but come out to help me."

A rustling inside the hut caused Kikongo to immediately drop to his knees with his forehead touching the ground. Slowly the door opened, and the witch doctor appeared. He took the chicken from the man who still kept his face to the ground. He inspected the bird closely for defects.

Apparently satisfied as to its health and youth, the witch doctor asked, "What is your trouble?"

"Ah, I have a bad girl. She refuses to marry the husband I have chosen for her. What can I do?"

The witch doctor made a guttural sound. Then he spoke. "That is easy. Punish her severely, and then you will see." He nodded his head sagely.

"Well," replied Kikongo dubiously, "I have beaten her. I have tried starving her, but nothing shakes her determination not to marry a heathen."

"Ha! Is that how it stands? I suppose she has been to the mission *eshuli* of the Seven days! Very good, I'll help you, and that without any extra pay except for this chicken. It is these schools that are undermining my power, making me poor. I have very special magic for disobedient girls. Here, take this potion and put it into her porridge tonight, and we'll see what effect it has on her," he said as he drew a pouch from under his filthy wrap-around cloth. He extracted a powder compounded of crushed lizard bone, dried snake blood, and ash, poured it into a section of bamboo, and then added some foul-smelling liquid to the concoction. "If for some reason my magic does not work because this girl has a charm from that school—you know these mission schools have very powerful magic—then you may return to me in a day or two, and we will go into the matter further."

Kikongo thanked the witch doctor profusely. And, satisfied that he would marry off his daughter according to plan, he departed. Stealthily he slipped the contents of the bamboo vial into Kimpayi's food, and then watched anxiously to see the effect it would have on her.

"This porridge has a very unpleasant smell," Kimpayi said as she took a bit of it to her mouth.

"Well, it could be that the cassava isn't as fresh as it might be. Mine doesn't taste too bad, and your father didn't seem to notice anything," the girl's mother soothed. "You had better finish your share, for you know your father doesn't want us to waste food."

Kikongo watched his daughter closely. The charm didn't seem to be having any visible effects on his daughter. He had expected she would start extolling the virtues of her future husband. When she said nothing he figured that perhaps it would take time for the *muti* [medicine] to take effect, so he waited till the next day to tell her that he had set the marriage date. "On Saturday morning Tembu will come to take you to the court to write up the marriage officially."

"You may drag me to the court, but I shall tell the *karani* [clerk] that I do not want to marry Tembu—and I shall *not* marry him." Kimpayi calmly told her father.

Kikongo went wild with anger. "You dare disobey me! We shall see," he screamed. He hit her head with his fists till she fell to the ground. Then he hurried off to the witch doctor.

"Your *muti* is useless," he accused the man.

"What do you mean?"

"I put your *muti* into Kimpayi's food last night and she ate it all, but this morning she still refused to marry Tembu. She even told me she would disgrace me before the court *karani*. Now what shall I do?"

"Bring her to me tomorrow. It might be a good idea if you fetch the future husband and bring them both to me. I may be able to work some special magic on the girl," the medicine man suggested.

Though not completely satisfied, the father returned home after first arranging with Tembu for him to visit his fiancée the following day.

"You are to come with me," commanded Kikongo the next morning.

"Are you taking me to the court? It will do you no good," warned his daughter.

"No, we are not taking you to the court—yet."

In silence the three set off through the forest till at last they reached the witch doctor's hut.

"Why will you not marry this man?" the witch doctor asked.

"He is a heathen and has two other wives, so I cannot marry him," the girl replied.

"Why can you not marry a heathen? Why have you become so foolish all of a sudden? If you do not marry him willingly we will force you to do it. If you are sensible we will reward you well," he continued.

"You cannot bribe me, nor can you intimidate me," she answered as she looked him fearlessly in the eye.

After he had exhausted all his arguments, the witch doctor, sensing that he was losing face before the two men, became infuriated. He picked up three hippohide whips and handed one to each of the men.

"Your father does not know how to treat you. Wait till you have tasted this medicine of mine; then you may speak differently," he said with an evil leer. "Do you think that you, a mere girl, can hold out against me, the greatest medicine man in Africa? We will whip you till you beg for mercy." With that he ripped off the cloth which was draped around the girl's body, and all three commenced flogging Kimpayi. First thick welts arose, then these split open, and the blood flowed freely down her back and legs. With satisfaction the men heard the groans she could not suppress.

"Now will you surrender? You deserve far more, but if you promise to obey, we will have mercy," shouted Kikongo.

"No, never. You may kill me, but I will not do what I know to be wrong. My Jesus suffered for me. I'm ready to die for Him," moaned the girl.

"Do you want a daughter that is no good to you? This girl is worse than useless. She is possessed of a strange devil that I do not know. My Black Magic is all that is left." The witch doctor gave a sinister, mirthless laugh. "That *may* help, but if it does not—then you will be well rid of such a worthless piece of goods." The witch doctor threw his weapon to the ground with disgust to wipe

91

away the sweat that streamed down his face.

"I suppose that is all we can do. Try your Black Magic on her. I will not have a daughter that is no use to me. All she does is eat up my money, giving me no returns. Let us not waste time but do as you suggest immediately," Kikongo agreed.

The three men dragged the half-conscious girl over to a huge tulip tree, tied her securely with her back against the rough bark, then rapped loudly on the trunk. The hollow sound rang through the forest. It was answered by an angry rustle from within which sent a shudder of terror through the girl. Almost immediately the huge, black driver ants swarmed out of a hole high up, in amongst the branches, and descending like lava out of a crater, they flowed over Kimpayi. The smell of blood from the wounds magnetized them. Deep into the tender flesh they bit. The hundreds of fiery bites drew fresh groans of agony from the girl.

"Now will you agree to marry Tembu?" mocked the witch doctor.

"Never! Oh, God, sustain me!" she prayed.

At the moment the young teacher of the mud-and-pole schoolhouse was hurrying through the forest on an errand. He stopped suddenly and listened. He hastened in the direction of the sounds, but even before he reached the spot, he knew what had happened. The imprecations hurled at the girl by the three demon-posssessed men told the story all too plainly. Peering through the dense foliage, he took in the scene at a glance. But what could he, one man alone, do? As if he had wings on his feet he sped back through the trees till he reached the home of Pastor Jonathan.

"Pastor, Pastor, come quickly. They are murdering Kimpayi."

Pastor Jonathan dropped what he was doing and hurried after the younger man, who had already turned and begun running back through the forest. As they ran the teacher told what he had seen.

"Pray God we will not be too late," said the pastor.

Into the midst of the group they dashed. Before the three men could lift a finger, the pastor had whipped out his large pocketknife and cut the vines with which the girl was tied. He carried her a little distance from the tree, laid her tenderly on the ground and began brushing the myriads of ants off the wounds while the teacher bent over her and pulled them out of her eyes, mouth, and nose. So quickly had it happened that the others had not had time to argue. But it did not take them long to find their voices.

"What business have you interfering with what we are doing?" shouted the witch doctor.

Without so much as looking up, the pastor continued removing the pinpoints of fire from the girl while he replied: "You inhuman creatures! Would you *kill* Kimpayi? It may well be that you have already done irreparable damage, but I am going to do my best to save her. She is one of my children."

"You lie! She is my daughter," screamed the father. "I can do what I like with her. She has disobeyed me, and now I am going to kill her the way I want to. Leave her alone that we may tie her to the tree so the ants can pick her bones clean."

"She is not your child any longer. You have forfeited all right to her, you wicked old man. She belongs to me, and I am going to take her to the hospital, and I shall report you three to the government. I know all about you. Kimpayi told me everything. We shall see what happens when I tell this story to the police."

Kikongo, Tembu, and the witch doctor had been advancing, rather irresolutely it is true, upon the two men bending over the unconscious girl, but when they heard the word *police* they shrank back.

"We were only trying to help her to obey her father," whined the witch doctor.

"I have no time for you now. If we do not get Kimpayi to the hospital soon, it will be too late. But don't think I am done with you," threatened the usually gentle pastor as he and the teacher picked up the limp girl and began hurrying in the direction of the hospital. After hours of running, walking stumbling, they eventually reached the hospital, where they gave Kimpayi into the care of the kindly nurses. Then they hastened to the police with their story.

"Take a policeman and fetch those three murderers—no take three policemen. If that girl dies, someone is going to pay for it," said the officer in charge.

For interminable days Kimpayi hovered in the valley of the shadow. It seemed she could not throw off the poison from the bites of the ferocious driver ants. For interminable days the three men sat in prison, hoping against hope that the one whom they had tried to kill would not die.

"If this girl dies, you will all three forfeit your lives to be an example for all others who might be tempted to do something similar," the officer said.

After much anxious, tender care, Kimpayi began slowly, miraculously, to recuperate. Weeks later she walked out of the hospital, healed and free. Personally she went and begged that those who had treated her so cruelly be pardoned.

"Girl, why did you not have us beaten, to say the least?" asked her father in astonishment.

"I have learned better things at the mission school," was her only answer.

No Real Regrets

The Missionary Mama's task at times seemed comparatively drab, while the Missionary Bwana went on safari and met people and saw results for his labors. Myrtle Campbell stayed on the mission and for the most part did more mundane tasks, while Rossier visited schools and preached in the villages. It was hard, too, to be so far from the homeland. Only at furlough-time could the missionary return to visit loved ones and family, for missionary salaries usually are not large enough to include the cost of a plane or steamship ticket to see loved relatives.

Mail to the Campbells came to the nearest little town once a week. A man walked to town to fetch it, at the same time taking the outgoing letters. Eagerly Myrtle and Rossier looked forward to mail day and letters from home.

One mail day a letter arrived from Myrtle's sister. She tore it open eagerly, only to drop it as she burst into tears.

"What's the matter?" Rossier asked anxiously.

"Dad's dead!"

"Oh, no! Why last week you had a letter from him and all was well. Here, let me see." He reached over and took the letter. "You're right. He's been dead a month and a half. Why must our mail take such ages to get here? My poor Myrtle!'' He held her close in his arms as he spoke.

After her sobs subsided, Rossier asked gently, ''Would you have liked to have gone home to him? Do you regret the sacrifice we made in coming to Africa? Maybe we should have gone back to help your dad after your mom died.''

Myrtle brushed away her tears. ''Regretted coming to Africa—no, never. My sister could look after Dad, though I do grieve that I could not help him—could not see him at the last. But I count it a precious privilege that God gave us the opportunity to help Christ find African diamonds to grace His crown.''

''Then we'll stay in Africa,'' Rossier said, ''seeking His diamonds as long as God wants us to; and when our work here is done, we'll hunt for diamonds in the homeland so we can hasten the day that O. J. Cushing aptly writes about in the song 'Jewels.' '' The chorus says:

> Like the stars of the morning,
> His bright crown adorning,
> They shall shine in their beauty,
> Bright gems for His crown.

Rossier wiped away a tear from Myrtle's cheek.

She tried to smile bravely through her tears. ''Thank you!'' she said softly. Then after a pause she added, ''How glad I am that we both took that class on missions so many, many years ago, the class that made us more missionary minded.''

And the tremulous smile on Myrtle's face told Rossier all he wanted to know.